THE BOAT OWNER'S GUIDE TO ENGINE INSTALLATION

THE BOAT OWNER'S GUIDE TO ENGINE INSTALLATION

PETER CAPLEN

Helmsman Books

First published in 1997 by
The Crowood Press Ltd
Ramsbury, Marlborough
Wiltshire SN8 2HR

British Library Cataloguing in Publication Data

A catalogue record for this book is available from the British Library.

ISBN 1 86126 090 3

Acknowledgements

My grateful thanks to Cummins Diesel for their help in the preparation of this book and much useful advice during the installation of the engine. Thanks also to Perkins Engines Ltd, for the supply of technical material and diagrams.

Typeset by MultiMedia Works Ltd, Gloucester
Printed and bound in Great Britain by WBC Book Manufacturers Ltd, Mid Glamorgan

CONTENTS

In memory of Rick, father, friend and co-builder of *Pershilla*, and our cats Blue, a Persian, and Shadow, a Chinchilla from whence the name *Pershilla* evolved.

INTRODUCTION

Any owner contemplating the installation of a new engine into a boat in preference to having it completed professionally is probably motivated by financial considerations. As with most boat work, engine installation is a labour-intensive and therefore costly operation. If it can be performed by the enthusiastic owner, it should result in large savings on labour costs; these savings can then be usefully spent on placating the owner's partner!

Installing an engine into a boat is not a job to be undertaken lightly. However, it is not unduly complicated or difficult, but the work must be performed correctly if the engine, and therefore the boat, is to have a long and trouble-free life. It does not matter whether the installation is in a new boat or a repowering project in an existing boat. In both cases the same basic care is required to ensure that the final result is successful from a performance point of view as well as being safe and reliable.

The DIY skills of the average owner/builder are quite adequate to complete the project, using mainly the normal repair and maintenance tools commonly found on board. It is surely fair to assume that the owner of a steel vessel will have access to welding equipment, while GRP enthusiasts will be familiar with moulding and bonding techniques using fibreglass materials, and owners of timber vessels

will be adept at woodwork. The only difference between engine installation and all the other myriad jobs to be performed by the DIY owner is the need to get the job absolutely right, and at the first attempt! There is only one way to ensure a satisfactory final outcome and that is careful planning through every stage of the job, from the initial choice of engine and gearbox through to the first sea trial.

This book is written as a practical guide to the work involved as performed in the real world. It will not explain how the job is done in a factory, working under controlled conditions to explicit drawings. It is based around the tools and skills of the average DIY enthusiast and the resourcefulness that we as a breed occasionally enjoy. The chapters are divided between explanations of the correct method of working and my own hands-on experience during a recent re-engining project.

There are several different reasons for installing a new engine into a boat. The most obvious occasion is when building a new boat, where the engine can be selected at an early stage of the building process. The engine room layout is then designed around the new engine.

The most straightforward type of engine change, on the other hand, is where a terminally damaged or worn-out engine is being replaced with a new or reconditioned unit of the same type and size. This simply entails swapping various parts between the old and new engine and installing the new unit into the mountings of the old. Although the manhandling of a heavy engine is always a problem, it should be the only problem in this situation.

Arguably the most complex engine replacement exercise is where a new engine totally different from the original is to be installed. There are three main occasions when this may be necessary: when replacing an uneconomical petrol engine with a diesel, when extra power is required for better performance, and in older vessels where the engine is worn out and obsolete, making a like-for-like replacement impossible.

Although we are concentrating mainly on repowering projects where the replacement engine is of a different make, type or size to the original, much of the work also applies to new installations and like-for-like replacements.

Whatever the size and type of boat and whether of steel, GRP or timber, the basic principles for installation are the same regardless of the make and power of the engine. The only differences are in the handling problems associated with lifting and manoeuvring heavy engines. Small engines can be installed by manually lifting them into place, but as size and weight increase so do the problems – and dangers – involved.

It is far easier to install an engine into a new boat than to repower an existing one as the engine compartment, engine beds and ancillary equipment are designed and installed to suit the engine. With an existing boat it is obligatory to work around the equipment and fittings that are already in place and this is where the greatest problems often lie. For this reason the planning stage is crucial. The space available may severely restrict the choice of engine and will almost certainly dictate the maximum physical size that can be practically accommodated.

It is not only the engine that has to be accommodated, moreover: problems can also arise with exhaust systems running through the accommodation, and propeller shafts that are of inadequate diameter to transmit the power and torque of the new engine.

To simplify the different aspects of the project, I have covered the work involved in three stages. The first four chapters deal with planning; Chapters 5 and 6 cover the preparation of the engine compartment to accept the new engine and the actual hands-on installation, while Chapters 7–11 examine the installation of the ancillary equipment associated with a new engine. The last chapter deals with running and testing the installed engine. By dividing the work up into three stages like this, difficulties can be foreseen and dealt with before they form obstacles to the smooth running of the project.

Although there will almost certainly be some grazed knuckles on the way, the work should be enjoyable and the satisfaction when the new engine bursts into life will have made the whole project very worthwhile.

I make no apologies for naming the companies that supplied equipment, parts and service for my own re-engining project as this book deals in specifics. These companies were all selected as part of the planning process and perfectly suited my own requirements. They may not suit other owners' requirements, who should follow the planning advice of section one.

My own vessel, *Pershilla*, is a 40ft De-Groot steel motor cruiser, home built from a standard kit of plates. By necessity she was completed on a very tight budget, and as is the case with many such projects her heart was a second-hand engine from the local commercial vehicle breakers. In this case it was an ex-truck six-cylinder Bedford 466 diesel producing 140 brake horsepower at 2,800rpm. Working on a finished displacement of 10 tons the power output of the Bedford would have provided *Pershilla* with a top speed of around 11 knots and a cruising speed of 10 knots. In the event her finished displacement was 14 tons, giving her a markedly inferior performance with a maximum speed of 9 knots and a consequent cruising speed of 8 knots. Although this engine took us several thousand fairly trouble-free miles, including a circumnavigation of Great Britain, *Pershilla* always felt underpowered. Several years later funds finally permitted the installation of a new, more powerful engine. Still needing to minimize costs I performed the installation myself with complete success.

TURBO-CHARGING

1

IS IT NECESSARY

When repowering for improved performance the first decision to be made concerns the actual performance required. Once that is established, it is fairly easy to calculate the power needed to provide that performance. The relationship between performance and power is fairly straightforward and engine suppliers will recommend suitable engine/s to provide the necessary power. With an idea of the power required the next decision should be whether to use a turbo-charged engine or a larger-capacity, naturally aspirated unit. There are advantages and disadvantages to turbo-charging and although this is a matter of personal preference I believe that the advantages outweigh the disadvantages.

For owners requiring modest power, say up to 80bhp, there is little need to opt for turbo-charging, as engines up to this capacity are quite moderate in size and can generally be accommodated without too many problems. In fact there are few marine engines in this power band that offer turbo-charging. For example, the lowest-powered Cummins diesel currently offering turbo-charging is 130bhp from a 3.9-litre block. The naturally aspirated version of this engine is 80bhp. Owners requiring engines in this lower power band can

therefore generally disregard the turbo-charging question.

For the express cruiser owner requiring ultimate power with diesel reliability a boosted diesel engine is the obvious choice. However, for the cruising owner there is also a lot to be said for choosing a turbo-charged engine. These engines are lighter and more compact for a given power output and they also have the additional advantage of improved fuel economy power for power over naturally aspirated diesels due to their inherent fuel efficiency.

Turbo-charging is all about how the engine breathes. A naturally aspirated engine simply breathes the air normally flowing into the cylinders induced by the induction (downwards) stroke of each piston. However, a turbo-charged engine is compelled to breathe the additional air that is forced into the cylinders under pressure from the turbo-charger. As the amount of air entering the cylinders is greater, the pressure within the combustion chamber on the compression stroke is also greater. When combined with the proportionally greater amount of atomized fuel injected into the combustion chamber the resulting burn provides greater power on the firing stroke.

Adding a turbo-charger to an engine provides a worthwhile increase in power with little increase in weight and only moderate expense. It therefore allows manufacturers to offer the same basic engine in a variety of power outputs to suit differing applications. Ideally the engine should be designed in the first instance to accept the additional pressure and running stresses of turbo-charging to ensure a long and trouble-free life. In reality, however, the base engine is designed first and foremost for turbo-charging and is then derated to the lower-powered, naturally aspirated version. As a matter of interest, this lower-powered version will probably have a commercial rating because of its heavy-duty construction. We will be looking in depth at duty cycles in Chapter 2.

To achieve diesel power-to-weight ratios approaching that of petrol engines the use of turbo-charging is now common practice, especially in the vehicle field. Whereas ten years ago turbo-chargers were only seen on high-performance cars and large trucks they are now increasingly used on both petrol and diesel cars for increased performance.

HOW IT WORKS

The word 'turbo-charger' derives from 'turbine', which is the basis of the turbo-charger. A turbine with vanes driven by the exhaust gases and rotating at up to 100,000 rpm is connected to a vane-type air pump that raises the pressure and volume of air entering the cylinders by amounts ranging from about 9 to 30lb depending on engine and designed use. As we have already seen, the increased pressure forces additional air into the cylinder, and coupled with the greater volume of atomized fuel, produces extra effort to the

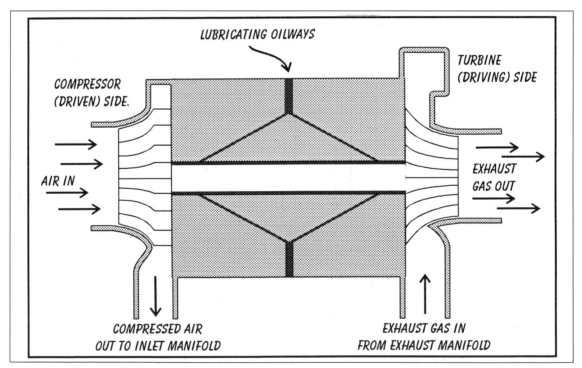

Cross-section through a turbo-charger.

piston on the downward combustion stroke, resulting in more power from the engine. Turbo-charging alone can increase the power of a standard engine by as much as 60 per cent, depending on the turbo pressure.

Unfortunately this increased pressure creates a problem of its own. It is well known that as air pressure increases, the temperature of the air also increases and this causes it to expand. A good example of heat generation in compressed air is demonstrated by placing a finger over the end of a bicycle pump and feeling the heat generated while pumping. This heat expansion prevents the full required charge of air from entering the cylinders and a stage is eventually reached where the turbo-charger is defeating its own object. The expanded air under pressure is no longer of greater volume than the unpressurized cool air. At this stage a charge air-cooler (or after-cooler or inter-cooler) is required if the power of the engine is to be boosted beyond the capabilities of the turbo-charger alone. The charge air-cooler cools the warm compressed air before it enters the cylinders. Cooling causes the air to contract, thus allowing a greater volume of air to enter the cylinder under turbo-charger pressure.

The additional air with the greater volume of atomized fuel provides a further increase in power over that provided by the turbo-charger alone. Charge air-coolers are similar in design to the standard heat exchanger used for engine water cooling although the concept is more akin to a car's radiator.

Cooling water circulates through a radiator-type matrix, over which the charge air passes on its way to the combustion chambers. Cooling may be achieved using either fresh water from the engine or raw water from the

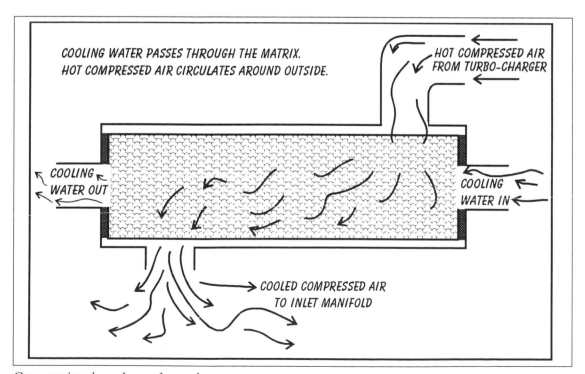

COOLING WATER PASSES THROUGH THE MATRIX. HOT COMPRESSED AIR CIRCULATES AROUND OUTSIDE.

HOT COMPRESSED AIR FROM TURBO-CHARGER

COOLING WATER OUT

COOLING WATER IN

COOLED COMPRESSED AIR TO INLET MANIFOLD

Cross-section through an after-cooler.

sea-water pump. To get an idea of just how 'warm' the charge air becomes, bear in mind that the fresh water from the engine used to cool this air is normally at around 80°C but still has a significant cooling effect.

The most effective level of cooling is clearly raw water. Usually passing through the after-cooler immediately after leaving the water pump while still cold, it noticeably reduces the temperature of the induction air and further increases power. Therefore even the type of after-cooler affects the power output of the engine.

DISADVANTAGES

Using a turbo-charger, charge air-cooler, modified pistons and fuel injection equipment can increase the power of an engine by over 100 per cent but the pressures on the engine are high and mean greater wear when used at full throttle. This makes it essential to conform to the manufacturer's specified duty cycle and match this with the correct service schedule and engine maintenance procedures as recommended by the manufacturer.

All engines require proper service at the specified intervals but for turbo-charged units servicing is even more critical. Oil and filter changes are particularly important as the close tolerances of the turbo-charger require clean oil at all times. It is also essential to use the correct grade of oil. This is usually of a higher grade and classification than for naturally aspirated engines.

Once a turbo-charger and after-cooler have been fitted, further power increases can only be achieved by reworking the internal design of the engine. High-performance and racing

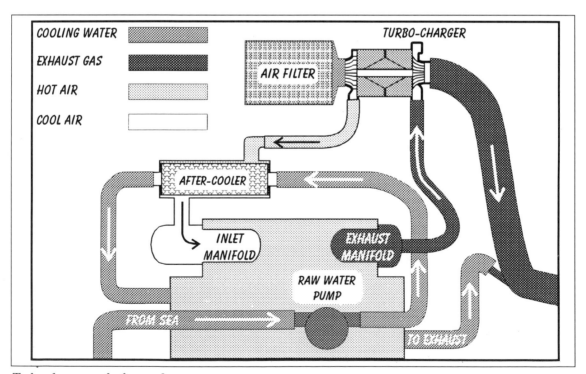

Turbo-charger and after-cooler arrangement.

engines are developed in this way. In extreme cases this very high performance leads to loss of reliability but for partially tuned sports boat engines, a modified duty cycle with greater restrictions on usage is the normal outcome. For the average cruising owner requiring reliability as well as performance a larger engine block with increased cubic capacity and modest turbo-charging is a much safer option than a lightweight turbo-charged sports boat engine. The other alternative is to choose a naturally aspirated engine that is heavier power for power and slightly less fuel-efficient, but has a higher duty rating.

2

PERFORMANCE AND POWER REQUIREMENTS

When repowering for improved performance the first decision to be made regards the actual performance and therefore speed required. Engine suppliers are usually able to recommend suitable engine/s to provide the required power. To give an accurate assessment of the necessary power, they will require various details of the vessel, including the water-line length, loaded displacement, and various other items of information that will vary between manufacturers.

SELECTING THE RIGHT ENGINE

The supplier will also need to know the proposed duty cycle of the vessel, or, in simple terms, what the vessel will be used for and how many hours per year it is expected to run. The duty cycle is designed to ensure that the engine enjoys a long and trouble-free life within the required operating environment and that wear and tear is at an acceptable level

Engines in this fast cruiser will have a pleasure/light commercial rating

A working boat will probably need engines with a medium continuous rating.

regardless of that environment. An engine required to work throughout its life at full power will be derated to relieve the stress of continual hard use. Commercial vessels such as tugs and pilot cutters are prime examples of this category. An engine in a pleasure craft only operating at weekends throughout the summer can be allowed to provide greater power for the relatively short time required of it as the additional wear from high-speed use is kept within acceptable limits. By balancing high speed and wear over short periods, against moderate wear over long periods, the overall life expectancy of both engines is similar.

Regardless of make, each basic engine model generally has at least three different duty ratings and each manufacturer's ratings are slightly different. Pleasure craft ratings generally provide the maximum power output, but only for a limited period. For example, full power use may be limited to one hour out of eight, while for continuous use the revs must be at least 200rpm below maximum.

On a cruising vessel maximum revs are rarely used so this is not a problem, and the continuously permitted maximum revs give the real usable horsepower available. Duty cycles also place a limit on the number of hours of annual operation of the engine and these again vary between manufacturers. However, as the running hours of the average motor vessel used for pleasure rarely exceeds 100 hours a year the figures are seldom critical. It is, however, essential to keep within the limits of the duty cycle during the warranty period of a new engine, otherwise the warranty may be deemed invalid if any problems arise.

The ideal place to begin a repowering project is at one of the national boat shows, where all the leading engine and ancillary suppliers are gathered together under one roof. This makes comparisons of performance, size and price very convenient.

The type of vessel is critical to the choice of engine and will decide not only the size and power but in many cases also the manufacturer. The reason for this is that some engine manufacturers now concentrate almost entirely on powering large sports cruisers. Concentrating on this area of the market, their engines are designed to provide very high power outputs from a relatively small capacity block. In practice this means they are highly stressed for most of their working lives and therefore have a light duty cycle specifically for planing craft. Being principally designed for this purpose, full power use is limited, making them unsuitable for long-distance cruising vessels. However, if the boat being repowered is a planing sports cruiser this type of engine is the ultimate choice for the rapid acceleration and high speed expected.

At the opposite end of the scale come the big-block, low-power 'sloggers', designed for working at full power twenty-four hours a day within a commercial environment. Long-distance cruising vessels may appear to come into this category, for, although not commercial vessels in the true sense, they will run continuously for long hours when on passage. However, except in very limited cases, the number of hours run annually is still likely to be within the bounds of the pleasure craft rating. There is little point in choosing a low-power, commercially rated engine unless it is to be used commercially on a daily basis. A higher-powered engine with a pleasure craft rating installed in a cruiser will offer similar levels of reliability to the commercially rated engine, just because it is always run at reduced revs while cruising. A good maxim to remember is that power does not have to be used just because it is available; nevertheless, it is there should it ever be required.

Manufacturers will advise on the specific engine models from their range to suit various types and size of vessel, while also allowing for the anticipated duty cycle. This advice is well worth heeding and is another very good reason for making initial enquiries at boat shows, where the experts can be quizzed face to face and their various claims and prices compared.

When considering performance requirements, top speed is generally less important than cruising speed. This may not apply to fast sports cruisers used exclusively for day trips and weekending where the thrill of high performance at maximum speed is the reason for ownership. For the cruising fraternity however, speed must be balanced against fuel economy when long passages are planned. Fuel consumption rises sharply as maximum vessel speed is approached, so cruising speed is the more important determinant of power required. It should be remembered that fuel consumption is similar between a low capacity engine running at full power and a high capacity engine running at cruising revs when both are producing the same brake horsepower, assuming that both engines are of the same design type. Fuel consumption does vary horsepower for horsepower between engines of different design and type regardless of manufacturer. Nevertheless, in general the design of any particular engine generally depends on its size and power output.

Full displacement cruisers whose top speed is limited by water-line length can happily use relatively low-powered engines to provide their maximum potential speed. In this case it would be a waste of money to buy a larger-capacity engine than was required to provide maximum speed. Ideally, the maximum economical speed of the vessel should be matched to the continuous maximum revs of the engine so that maximum cruising speed can be maintained without having to worry about over-stressing the engine or draining the fuel tanks too rapidly. In practice it is possible to push a full displacement cruiser a little beyond her theoretical maximum speed but this takes huge amounts of power and even larger amounts of fuel. Taking this to extreme lengths, if the power was available it could take five extra gallons of fuel per hour to increase speed by 0.1 knots. This would not only be a waste of resources but also a dangerous situation to put the vessel into, as the stern would be progressively forced down, making her unstable. With unlimited power it is theoretically possible for a displacement vessel to sink herself by the stern.

From this extreme example it is clear that owners looking to repower full displacement cruisers will not require the type of power output that owners of planing and semi-planing vessels may want. However, it is not compulsory for planing and semi-planing craft to achieve their designed hull speed and many owners of this style of vessel, especially those with river moorings, are very happy to cruise at displacement speed with low-powered engines for the sake of economy.

The alternative point of view is based on the maxim mentioned above: 'Just because the power is available, it does not have to be used, but it is there should it be required.' Although the choice is always up to the individual, a good maxim with planing and semi-planing vessels is to install the largest engines that the budget will permit and that are safely within the bounds of the vessel's capabilities. This provides the best of all worlds and was the repowering option I took with *Pershilla*.

Owing to *Pershilla*'s displacement and long-range cruising potential I was looking for an engine with a duty cycle between the two extremes of light-duty pleasure and heavy-duty commercial. There are usually several options between these two limits, covering all types of craft. For a heavy cruising boat like *Pershilla* the pleasure/light commercial rating covered my needs. In addition to selecting the right duty cycle I was also looking for a modern engine design with a favourable power to weight ratio that would be easy to repair without requiring the use of specialized tools. Another essential was that it should utilize the same base engine parts as truck versions, thus making it possible to buy parts over the counter at the local truck dealer's rather than having to pay a heavy additional premium for the word 'Marine' on the box.

THE GEARBOX

Having selected the engine the next major decision is the gearbox. The choice of manufacturer is up to the individual, and in the smaller capacity range there is nothing further to be decided than the appropriate model to suit the engine. For twin-engine installations there are a couple of additional points to note when deciding on gearbox maker. The first is whether the standard gearbox can run at full rated speed in forward and reverse to provide contra-rotation of the propellers or whether different models of gearbox must be ordered.

Contra-rotating propellers (starboard propeller turning clockwise when viewed from aft, port propeller turning anticlockwise) provide the best performance as each cancels out the 'paddle wheel' effect of the other to provide straight-line running with no rudder correction. The second consideration is whether the reduction ratios are identical in forward and reverse or whether – as in some cases – they are slightly different and therefore require

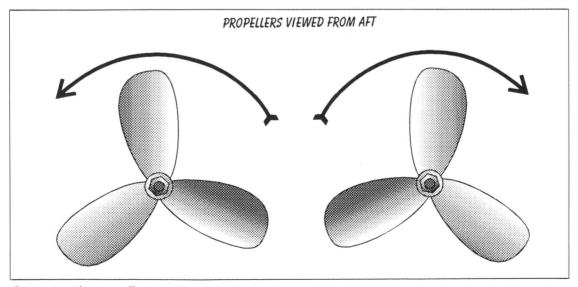

PROPELLERS VIEWED FROM AFT

Contra-rotating propellers.

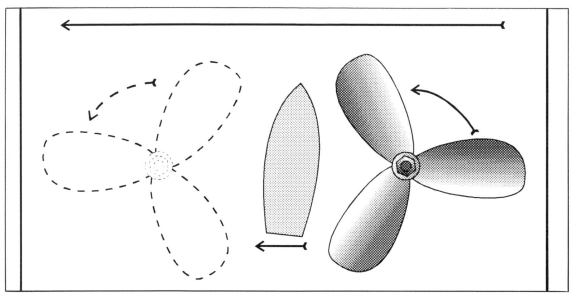

Paddle-wheel effect. In this case a left-hand propeller running anticlockwise 'wheels' the stern to port, causing the vessel to turn to starboard. This tendency is corrected using rudder offset in the opposite direction.

different-sized propellers. With differing propeller sizes a slight thrust imbalance is produced for a given engine speed. This in itself is not a big problem but it is always preferable to keep the gearbox ratios and the propeller sizes equal if at all possible.

Type of Gearbox

In the larger-capacity engine range there is less choice of gearbox manufacturer than for the smaller engines. When matching a gearbox to an engine with power output greater than about 250bhp, boxes robust enough to handle the torque produced at the relatively low revs of even modern diesel engines are not available from every manufacturer. I visited every gearbox manufacturer at the London Boat Show but only a couple could provide a gearbox to handle the required power output and torque. One company that did have a suitable box only produced it with a 10-degree down-angle output shaft. This would have

been ideal in a new boat as the down-angle allows the engine to be installed horizontally in the engine compartment instead of in-line with the propeller shaft. This arrangement substantially reduces the headroom required in the engine compartment and can be an important requirement where the engines are located below the wheelhouse floor. However, in *Pershilla* the engine beds were already installed in the traditional manner and the work that would have been required to remake the beds for a retro-fit made that particular gearbox an impractical proposition.

In other circumstances a down-angle gearbox may be the only option, depending on the angle of the propeller shaft and the allowed engine installation angle. Every engine has a maximum angle at which it can be installed to allow proper oil pick-up and circulation. If the installation angle is too steep, a down-angle gearbox or universal joint coupling such as the Aqua-Drive may be the only option to allow the engine to be installed at the permitted

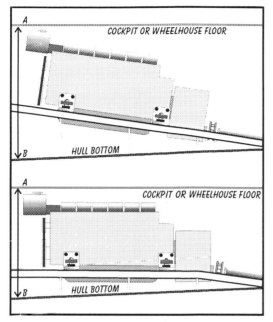

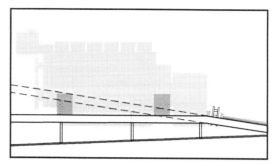

If a down-angle gearbox is used for a retro-installation, the original engine beds (dotted) will normally have to be cut away and new lower beds built.

By using a down-angle gearbox (bottom) in preference to a standard model (top) the height of the cockpit or wheelhouse floor (A–B) can be reduced by up to 20 per cent.

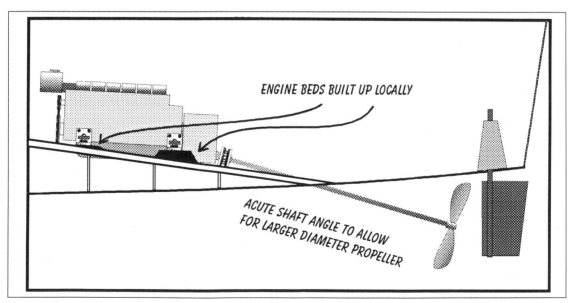

Where the propeller shaft angle must be changed to accept a larger diameter propeller it is often possible to modify the original beds by building up locally to suit a down-angle gearbox.

The Aqua-Drive universal joint shaft coupling from Halyard Marine.

angle. At the opposite end of the scale, engines are almost never installed nose down except under very specialized conditions and after consultation with the manufacturer, who may need to modify the engine prior to installation. Whatever the type of gearbox finally chosen, once into the higher horsepower brackets it soon becomes necessary to look at commercially rated gearboxes to accommodate the power output.

Reduction Ratio

The make and type of gearbox is only the first part of the decision. The next factor is the reduction ratio, that is, the difference between the output speed of the engine at the flywheel and the required speed of the propeller shaft. In very simple terms a slow-revving propeller gives much greater thrust for a heavy cruising boat while a high-revving propeller provides the rapid acceleration required by a sports cruiser. Although the slow-revving propeller is more efficient for moving heavy boats, the slower speed requires more blade area to produce the thrust required to move the boat while at the same time avoiding cavitation.

In one sense this simplifies matters as there is a practical limit to the maximum size of propeller that can be accommodated under the boat, and this decides the maximum practical reduction ratio. In simple terms a slow, heavy boat benefits from a high reduction ratio. The 3:1 ratio where, for example, the engine revs at 2,400rpm and the propeller shaft revolves at 800rpm is often chosen as a compromise between the need for a slow-revving propeller and the propeller size limitations imposed by the vessel's underwater design. Fast, heavy boats still require the large blade area but may need more revs and therefore a smaller reduction ratio. Light planing vessels prefer more revs at the propeller and will often have a direct drive gearbox or a minimal 1.5:1 reduction ratio. As the reduction ratio decreases so too does the output torque, making it possible to use lighter and less robust gearboxes.

Drop

But this is not the end of the story. A further complication in the gearbox selection process concerns the vertical distance between the gearbox input shaft (in line with the engine crankshaft) and the output shaft (coupled to the propeller shaft). This is known as the 'drop' and varies between gearbox manufacturers and gearbox models. It must be taken into account as it forms the junction between the engine and the propeller shaft. Some gearboxes have a straight-through arrangement where there is no drop, but these are generally only found on smaller boxes. Another option is the 'V' drive gearbox. This box has its input and output shafts one below the other on the same side of the casing. In this case the engine can be mounted right aft over the propeller shaft. The advantage of this system is that the engines can be installed well aft, out of the accommodation, in the same manner as when using outdrives but without the problems and vulnerability associated with them.

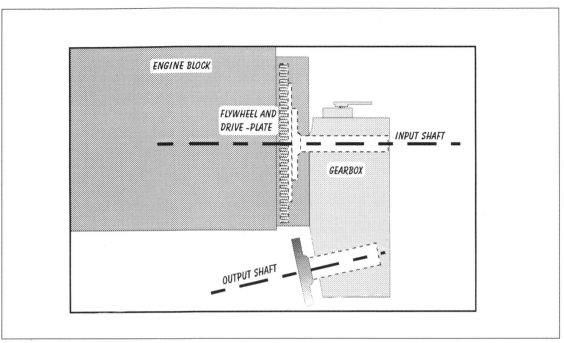

A 'V' drive gearbox allows the engine to be installed over the propeller shaft right aft.

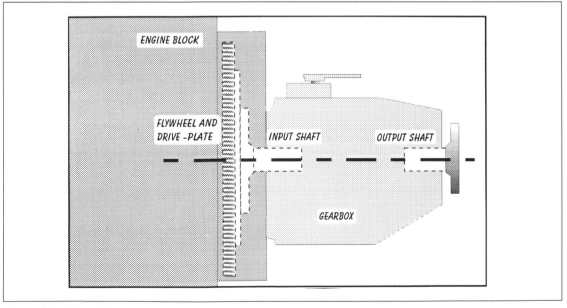

A 'straight-through' gearbox with no drop.

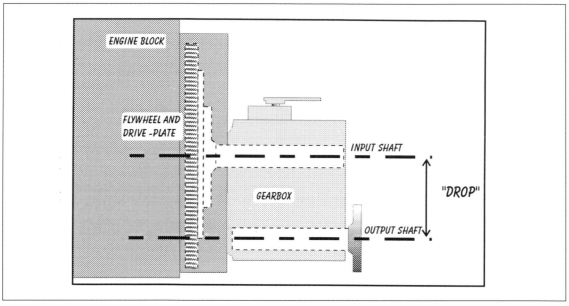

Gearbox drop. The vertical distance between the engine crankshaft (gearbox input shaft) and the gearbox output shaft.

THE PROPELLER

On a repowering project the drop decides the installed height of the engine, since, with the propeller shaft already installed, the engine height is the only variable. On a new build installation the two components, propeller shaft position and installed engine height, can be adjusted to suit the vessel's layout and design. Having looked at the myriad possibilities in gearbox design, propeller size once again enters the equation. This is an area where professional advice is invaluable and a good source of information is the propeller manufacturer. Nowadays most propeller calculations are made using computers that not only provide the propeller size and pitch but also calculate the optimum reduction ratio for maximum performance with any given type of boat. By feeding in different combinations of engine power, gearbox reduction ratio and maximum practical propeller size the optimum combination can

be calculated. It is almost essential therefore to check with your chosen propeller supplier before deciding on the optimum reduction ratio.

A further piece of critical advice that the propeller manufacturer can supply is the minimum diameter propeller shaft required to transmit the power using the chosen reduction ratio without twisting. Increased power may require a larger diameter propeller shaft, as may a greater reduction ratio. A combination of the two will make this a certainty. In some cases the propeller shaft diameter will be the ultimate factor in deciding engine power.

Pershilla, for example, has a propeller shaft of 1¾in. This was fine for the Bedford with 140hp even when I increased the reduction ratio to 3:1 in a bid to improve performance a few years ago. To contemplate more than doubling the power would have meant that the currently installed shaft would very soon have begun twisting into a spiral when under load. The shaft runs in bearings within a steel tube welded at the top and bottom into the centre keel. To increase the propeller shaft diameter would have meant cutting out the tube and replacing it with a larger diameter tube to accommodate the new shaft – an immensely difficult and time-consuming job that would have made the project uneconomical.

Luckily there is now an alternative available in the form of high-strength alloy shafts. These were originally devised to allow smaller diameter shafts and struts to be fitted on high-speed craft to cut down on the drag through the water caused by large-proportioned stern gear.

Size for size these high-strength alloy shafts can handle much greater power than the standard 316 grade stainless steel shaft and as an added bonus the very highest grades are totally corrosion free. They cost perhaps twice the price of a stainless steel shaft but even this is preferable to (and cheaper than) the alternative of replacing the entire shaft assembly. The additional cost could almost be justified by the corrosion-free nature of the material as 316 grade stainless steel has peculiar corrosion problems all of its own.

THE EXHAUST SYSTEM

The last major item of equipment to be considered is the exhaust system. A larger engine will inevitably require a larger bore exhaust system and this can create major installation problems depending on the layout of the vessel. As soon as the make and model of engine has been decided the required exhaust size can be ascertained and the extent of the problems, if any, can be gauged. In general terms, a 150hp engine will require a 3in exhaust while a 300hp engine will need a 6in one.

A critical factor with turbo-charged engines is back pressure within the exhaust. If not kept to within reasonable limits, back pressure will restrict the speed of the turbo-charger, preventing the engine producing full power and creating clouds of exhaust smoke due to insufficient air entering the cylinders.

It would be easy to think that the installation of two 3in exhausts would be the same as installing one 6in one. Of course in practice this does not work, as the area of a 3in exhaust is 7.0686sq. in while the area of a 6in exhaust is 28.2744sq. in, exactly four times greater. However, although a larger diameter circular exhaust may be a problem to fit, it may not be necessary to use a circular shape at all. As long as the internal area is the same as that of the required tube size there will be no problems with back pressure. It may therefore

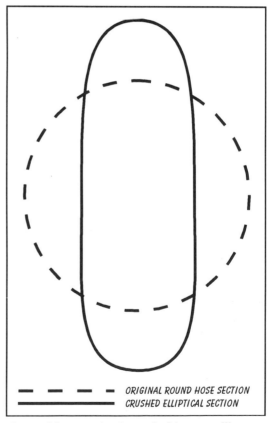

— — — — ORIGINAL ROUND HOSE SECTION
———————— CRUSHED ELLIPTICAL SECTION

A round hose section is crushed into an ellipse, but the internal area remains the same.

be possible to use an oval or box section to restrict the width and prevent the exhaust encroaching too far into the accommodation.

A further potential cause of back pressure is created by silencers, which may make it necessary to increase the size of the exhaust pipework yet again to provide a free flow of gases. I think that a silencer is an essential part of the system as the drone of an unsilenced exhaust can become very tedious after many hours of cruising. Once again this is an area where expert advice will be very valuable and will help to avoid problems with both noise and performance.

ANCILLARY PARTS

There are other vital ancillary parts to be selected before the planning is finalized. The cooling system will almost certainly need to be uprated when a larger engine is installed, beginning with the raw-water inlet skin fitting, through the raw-water strainer and of course the size of the pipework itself. The engine installation manual should provide details of the size of each part of the system but as a general rule the raw-water pump pipe fittings are the same size as the pipework. For example a water pump with $1^1/_2$in pipe fittings will require pipework of the same size. The raw-water strainer will also have the same size fittings and a water capacity to match.

The fuel system may similarly need uprating, with larger-bore pipework and higher-capacity filters. If in doubt it is better to fit the largest filter units possible to ensure an excess of capacity rather than risk restricting the fuel flow. Fitting larger-capacity filters also helps to prevent filter blockage in rough weather, when dirt in a contaminated tank is stirred up.

The electrical system probably requires the least modification, although a new engine will almost certainly be accompanied by a new set of instruments that will need fitting into the original instrument panel. Many engine manufacturers provide a complete instrument set ready mounted into a panel. My experience is that these panels rarely suit the layout of an established vessel's instrument panel and I prefer to incorporate the separate instruments into the vessel's own panel. In the case of a newly built boat a smart engine panel may be included in the design of the helm area but for a retro-fit it is usually easier to install the instruments separately.

Still on the electrical system, the starter cable may need uprating to take the extra current required to start a large capacity engine. The batteries may also be underrated. This will almost certainly be the case when changing from petrol to diesel because a more powerful starter motor is required to overcome the higher compression of the diesel. The battery isolation switch should not be forgotten as this may also be undersized for the current draw of a large engine.

3

PUTTING IT ALL TOGETHER

Having weighed up all the options discussed in the previous two chapters, it is now time to make the final decisions. The make, size and power of the new engine have to be decided on first, closely followed by a choice of gearbox to suit both the engine and the boat.

My own choice of machinery was made after carefully weighing up all the factors discussed while also bearing in mind that I was working within a tight budget. However, as it transpired, it was possible to specify top brand equipment throughout the project without greatly exceeding the budget. I doubt I could have improved on any aspect of the work even with an unlimited budget.

I must stress that what suited my own needs

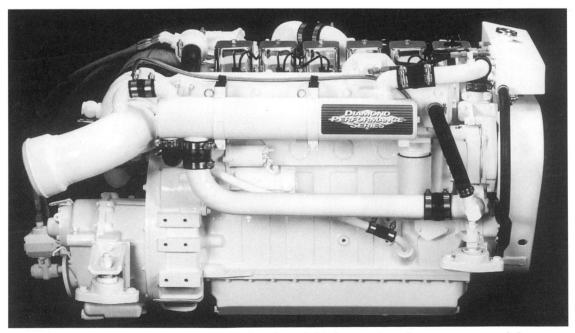

Cummins B series engine with 5.9-litre block and available in a variety of power outputs and duty ratings.

may not suit others. It is vital that each component is chosen to suit the specific needs of the vessel and the owner's aspirations before finalizing the decision to buy any particular make and type of machinery. Every owner will have their own individual set of criteria on which to base their choice of engine. Some owners may prefer to have an engine supplied by an agent within their own marina, making warranty work and spare parts very convenient. Others will be loyal to a particular maker through long years of quality service and reliable engine performance, while some will want economically priced spares available from a world-wide dealer network.

PERSHILLA

The Engine Itself

The following simply recounts my personal choice of engine and gearbox and the reasons

behind the decisions taken. The choice of engine manufacturer was finally narrowed down to the American company Cummins, who neatly encompassed all my requirements. They had recently uprated their 'small' engine range of 6- and 8-litre B and C series engines. The marque is famous in the shipping world for large marine engines that power ships and also has an excellent reputation within the road transport industry. As a bonus I then discovered that Cummins could offer one of the best warranty schemes in the business, with two years' cover on parts and labour plus three years on major parts. The standard finish of gleaming white paint and chromium-plated rocker covers, header tank and heat exchanger hardly influenced me at all!

After much discussion, the Cummins engine chosen for *Pershilla* was a B series 6BTA M2. This engine produces 300 brake horsepower at 2,800rpm from a turbo-charged and raw-water, inter-cooled 5.9-litre, six-cylinder block. This was clearly a big step up

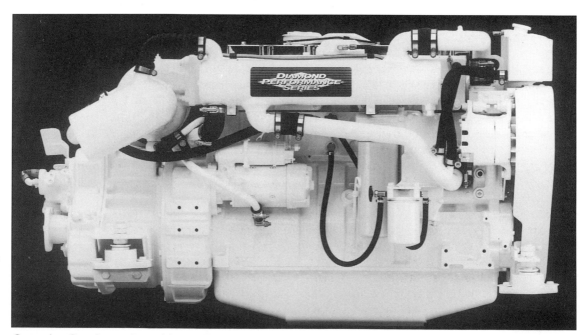

Cummins C series engine with 8.3-litre block, also available with differing power and duty ratings.

from the 140 brake horsepower of the Bedford and was expected to provide a maximum speed of over 12 knots with constant cruising at 11 knots. The Cummins recreational duty cycle also more than adequately covered my cruising aspirations for the foreseeable future. Full power running at maximum revs is available for one hour out of eight, with continuous cruising at 200rpm below maximum and a realistic limit of 750 hours' running a year.

With this decision provisionally made I took a Cummins installation drawing of the engine and made detailed measurements within *Pershilla*'s engine compartment to ensure that the engine would fit. I assumed that the output shaft drop of the new gearbox would be similar to that of the box on the Bedford, and made my calculations allowing for some slight difference between makers.

The engine itself, being a 5.9-litre rather than a 7.25-litre like the Bedford block, was physically smaller than the Bedford. However, the amount of additional equipment hanging on the engine in the form of turbo-charger, after-cooler and associated pipework made it several inches wider. The position of the engine mounting feet was both higher and narrower than on the Bedford although overall the engine was about 25 per cent lighter. I was pleased to find that the extreme top of the engine was no higher than the Bedford and that it could be accommodated below the wheelhouse floor without any modifications being necessary. The extra width of the engine ancillaries was the only problem I could find on the first assessment, and this could be overcome by cutting out the steel floor supports and moving each of them outwards about 2in (5cm). It also became clear that it would be necessary to remove some of the Cummins engine ancillaries before the engine was lifted in and then refit them *in situ*.

As the mounting feet were higher on the Cummins than on the Bedford I could see no major problems there. Had the mounting feet been lower, there would have been a great deal of extra work required, cutting out and lowering the beds. Raising them was simply a matter of building them up. Other than these two points I was pleased that the choice of engine was not raising any major problems; it all looked pretty straightforward.

The Gearbox

The next step was to choose the gearbox and this was when I became aware of the problem of finding a box strong enough to handle the power. After much deliberation I went back to Cummins and asked what their preferred choice of gearbox would be. They recommended Twin Disc, one of their preferred standard suppliers. Twin Disc produce high-quality gearboxes for the commercial and luxury motor-yacht market and although the price was stretching my budget to the limit I could not see any other option. In any case I consoled myself with the fact that I would be buying a top-quality product.

Before going any further I contacted several propeller makers for propeller calculations and costs. I also asked for a calculation of the optimum reduction ratio, and as I suspected this was unanimously agreed upon as 3:1. I next contacted the local UK agents for Twin Disc, who specified a MG 5061 with 3:1 reduction ratio as the standard fit for the 300bhp Cummins B series. They also mentioned that the normal procedure was to ship the box directly to Cummins for installation onto the engine thus saving me some additional work. Although they had no qualms about supplying the box directly to me for fitting I was very happy to avoid having to manhandle a 220lb (100kg) gearbox into accurate alignment with the engine drive plate. Having ascertained that the output shaft drop of this gearbox was indeed within the bounds of my initial calculations, I returned to *Pershilla* and rechecked everything, this time including the actual gearbox dimensions in the examination.

After ensuring that this gearbox would fit into the compartment with the engine I was then able to take more detailed measurements and plan the final position of the engine in the fore and aft line in relation to where the propeller shaft would couple to the gearbox. With this position decided, I could accurately calculate how much of each of the wheelhouse floor supports would need to be cut out and how far each one would actually need to be moved.

The Exhaust

At this stage I was already looking to keep modification work to the absolute minimum. For a re-engining project the less that has to be altered the better. Unfortunately, as the difference in size between the old and new engines increases, so does the amount of rebuilding work within the engine compartment and the number of ancillary parts.

For example, the exhaust system on *Pershilla*'s Bedford engine utilized a standard 3in rubber exhaust hose that ran via a Vetus water-lock silencer installed close to the engine within the confines of the engine compartment. From the silencer the exhaust was run through the aft engine-room bulkhead via a home-made steel, flanged, watertight fitting. It then ran a tortuous route around the back of a locker and four-drawer cabinet, down the starboard side of the aft cabin and under the double bed. It finally exited through the transom via a Vetus rubber transom fitting behind the enclosed headboard of the bed. The original exhaust was installed during the building of *Pershilla* and the furniture was then more or less built over it.

The recommended minimum wet exhaust size for the Cummins was 5in, nearly three times the cross-sectional area of the Bedford exhaust. Nevertheless, at this stage, being fired with enthusiasm for the new engine, I was prepared for a lot of rebuilding in the aft cabin if this was necessary. I briefly considered running the exhaust directly out through the side of the engine compartment, but soon rejected this as I have never been keen on this arrangement due to the possibility of fumes entering the accommodation, both when stationary and under way.

Bearing in mind the problems of back pressure I contacted Halyard Marine for their advice on the best way to run the exhaust through to the transom. With a roughly dimensioned drawing of the layout of the boat and the exhaust run they were able to offer several different options. The latest water separation system allows the use of smaller bore piping as the water is removed from the exhaust via a separator after leaving the lift silencer. Using this system means that the exhaust gases are cooled sufficiently to flow safely through the rubber exhaust hose dry. This system has become very popular for use with water-cooled generators as it removes the annoying 'sploshing' sound of water from the exhaust when running the generator at night.

However, as this system is slightly more expensive I opted for a standard system with the whole pipe-run being water-cooled. With this decision made, Halyard specified the exact size of silencer to match the engine and length of the exhaust pipework. Due to the overall length of the exhaust, a 6in hose was specified for the run from the silencer, located in the engine compartment, to the transom. From the engine to the silencer, 5in hose was specified to suit the standard exhaust outlet of the Cummins. This layout would provide the necessary silencing without producing any back-pressure problems.

The Propeller

Another major item on the shopping list was a propeller to match the new engine. Many people place little importance on the propeller and are quite happy to use something found at a boat jumble that is 'almost' the right size. However, the propeller is the most crucial part of the power transmission system. It must be the right diameter and have the correct blade area to provide the necessary thrust without cavitation, while having the correct pitch to match the power output of the engine.

As mentioned earlier, the $1^3/4$in diameter propeller shaft used for the Bedford was not strong enough to transmit the power of the new engine without twisting and would be uneconomical to cut out and replace with a larger size. After making enquiries and receiving several different quotations I tried CJR Propulsion, whose prices were very competitive and whose propellers had recently been fitted on a friend's new 52ft De-Groot, giving excellent smooth running performance.

They offered two grades of shafting apart from the standard 316 grade stainless steel. The brand names of the high-strength alloys are 'Marinemet 17' and 'Marinemet 22'; both could handle the power, but only the top grade '22' was corrosion-free. This was the obvious choice and although twice the price of stainless steel, was very much cheaper than the cost of installing a new propeller shaft tube. On CJR's recommendation, the shaft was ordered with matching tapers either end so that when it eventually shows signs of wear it can simply be reversed, thereby doubling the effective life.

An unmachined gearbox half-coupling is supplied from Twin Disc with the box but was not suitable for boring to suit the reversible shaft so a new coupling was supplied by CJR. They also supplied the R & D flexible coupling and a one-off Cutless bearing for the outer end of the propeller shaft tube. The propeller-calculating computer recommended a 28in diameter x $28^1/2$in pitch four-bladed propeller, which sounded about right when compared with the 29 X 20 three-blade used on the Bedford. As propeller calculation is still an imprecise science despite the advent of the computer, the accuracy of this calculation could not be proven until sea trials began.

A Place to Work

The final requirement of a project such as this, while not really being an ancillary component, is a suitable location to carry out the actual work. Depending on the engine size involved, a means of lifting out the old engine and lifting in the new could be an important requirement. Another could be access to willing helpers when required. For most people this means doing the job in a boatyard or marina. Over the years I have used all sorts of methods for lifting out engines. Mooring under a footbridge and hoisting the engine using a tackle lashed to the bridge was fairly successful; getting seven or eight unwitting helpers to haul half a ton of iron up a scaffold board was less enjoyable. In the end it is far better and safer to accept the slight extra expense and use a crane to lift heavy engines. Believe me, I know this from experience! This is especially true when dealing with several thousand pounds worth of new engine and gearbox.

Pershilla had been based at Gillingham Marina on the Medway for the last eight years and the workshop and staff have an excellent reputation with customers. The yard staff have always been friendly and helpful and with the back-up of the workshop staff I had no qualms about completing the job in the DIY yard there and using the crane mounted on the travel-lift for hoisting purposes. In the event it was a decision well made.

4

STERN GEAR AND ENGINE BEDS

Although still in the planning stage it is important to look at engine bed and stern gear installation. In some cases extensive modifications will be needed to the vessel to accommodate the new engine. Where this involves installing new stern gear and engine beds, the angle of these in relation to the water-line may affect the choice of gearbox or require the use of a universal joint coupling.

The choice of stern gear depends very much on the design of the vessel. We have already looked at the high-strength alloys that allow smaller shaft diameters to accept greater power without twisting. The additional cost of one of these shafts over a standard 316 grade shaft is probably no more than the cost of converting the stern tube and shaft bracket to a larger size, and certainly means a great deal

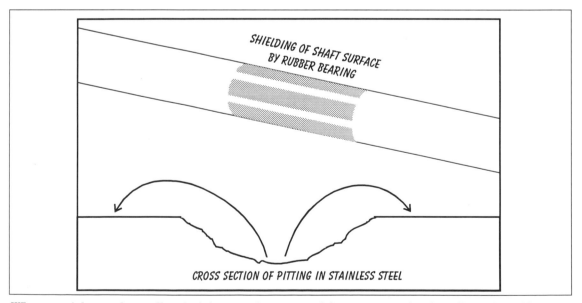

SHIELDING OF SHAFT SURFACE BY RUBBER BEARING

CROSS SECTION OF PITTING IN STAINLESS STEEL

When a stainless steel propeller shaft in water is not turned for many months, the splines of a rubber bearing can shield the surface of the shaft and starve it of its oxygen layer. Without the protective oxygen layer, surface pitting may commence.

less work. The other huge advantage is the corrosion resistance of the highest grades.

The usual grade of stainless steel used for propeller shafts is 316; the lower 304 grade is occasionally used but is even less corrosion-resistant and does not warrant the difference in cost. Although 316 stainless steel has generally good corrosion resistance, it relies on a layer of oxygen covering the entire surface of the metal to maintain its resistance. If an area of the shaft is shielded so that the surface is deprived of its oxygen, layer pitting erosion can be set up. For example, if rubber shaft bearings are used and the shaft is not turned for several months, the splines of the bearing will press onto the shaft, shielding it. Another cause of shielding is the humble barnacle. If left on the shaft for several months this can also produce the necessary conditions for pitting erosion.

Once pitting begins the process continues whether or not the surface has a layer of oxygen, as the metal within the pit is lower down the galvanic scale than that of the surrounding unpitted metal. The extent of the problem may depend on other factors apart from the shielding of the metal surface. For example, a shaft with good anodes will suffer less than an unprotected shaft, and corrosion is always less likely to occur on a well-used and well-maintained boat than one that is neglected for months on end. Nevertheless it is another very good reason for choosing one of the modern high-strength alloys.

Both the material and diameter of the propeller shaft will affect the number of shaft bearings required for a set length of shaft, and so to a lesser extent will the engine power and reduction ratio of the gearbox, as both of these factors contribute to the speed of the shaft. The material and diameter together will determine whether the shaft will twist due to the torque of the engine and gearbox reduction; these two factors also determine how good the shaft is at absorbing the wear

and stress caused when hitting underwater obstructions. The correct number of bearings prevent shaft whip at high shaft revs on long shaft lengths.

ENGINE BED ALIGNMENT

The method of constructing engine beds and aligning them with the propeller shaft is a subject of interest to both repowering and new build owners. Hopefully a repowering project will not require a total rebuild of the engine beds and stern gear. Unfortunately in some cases there may be no other option than to make radical changes to the boat to enable larger engines to be installed. The most likely reason for radical change is insufficient space between the hull and propeller shaft to accommodate the radius of the required propeller. Where the problem is slight the propeller manufacturer will often be able to redesign the propeller with a smaller diameter and compensate for this with greater blade area and pitch. Where the change required is very large, the only solution is to lower the outboard end of the shaft by increasing the angle at which it passes through the hull.

Unfortunately the radical difference between the old and new propeller sizes may make the increased shaft angle too great to allow the engine beds to be realigned. As we have already seen, every engine has a maximum installation angle that must not be exceeded due to the design of the oil pick-up in the sump. In this case the work may be greatly simplified by using a down-angle gearbox. This will almost certainly provide the additional angle required to accommodate the new shaft attitude without making significant alterations to the engine beds necessary beyond minor reshimming during final coupling alignment.

As some projects will inevitably require complete rebuilding of the engine beds the

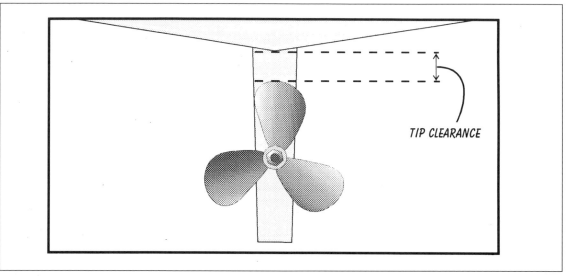

The correct minimum propeller tip clearance is essential to prevent rumblings and vibration from the aft sections of the vessel.

basic methods of setting up propeller shaft and engine bed alignment are described as for a new build. When a new shell is being fitted out the moulders usually provide the dimensioned drawings required to make shaft and engine bed alignment easy. They may also provide ready-made shaft brackets and steel engine-mounting frames. Then again they may not, and it is then up to the owner to set up the beds and shaft brackets.

Positioning the Propeller Shaft

This is one of those jobs that appears complicated but is really no more complex than a piece of string. And string is one of the main tools of the job! The first essential is to find the distance between the bottom of the boat and the centre of the propeller shaft at the point where the propeller is fitted. This is to allow for propeller tip clearance beneath the hull. Greater clearance cuts down on propeller noise, although acceptable minimum clearance varies between boats. Slow-revving

propellers can generally be permitted less clearance than fast-revving ones, but in all cases it is best practice to make the propeller tip clearance as large as possible with regard to any other restricting feature. To find the distance between the bottom of the boat and the centre of the propeller shaft, add 15 per cent of the propeller diameter to the radius as a good average tip clearance.

> ### Example
>
> 25in diameter propeller = 12.5in radius
>
> 25 x 15% = 3.75in tip clearance
>
> 12.5in radius + 3.75in tip clearance = 16.25in required between hull bottom and shaft centre

For a single-engine vessel the propeller shaft is obviously on the centre-line. For a twin-engine vessel each engine will be placed roughly a third of the beam in from each side. There is some room for leeway in this

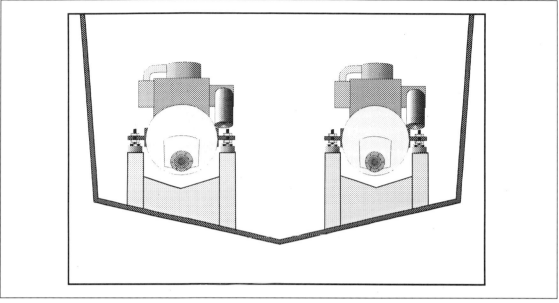

Twin engines will be positioned approximately a third of the beam in from each side, but the final positioning is decided by individual hull design.

position, but the shape of the hull and the amount of room required for maintenance must be taken into account. The following description is for a single-engine vessel; simply carry out the procedure twice for twin engines.

Assuming there are no drawings to work from, the first step is to find the position of the centre of the propeller shaft at the propeller end. This position should be forward of the rudder, allowing as much clearance as possible between the rudder and propeller. It is easiest to visualize the final installation by making a rough mock-up of the shaft bracket to the appropriate size to suit the propeller diameter and tip clearance. A piece of ply taped to the underside of the hull is quite adequate as long as it is firmly mounted. The spot where the shaft will pass through the hull can next be marked after taking into account the proposed position of the engine within the hull. At this stage some 'guesstimation' is allowed as only a rough idea of where the shaft passes through

the hull is needed. Once the first hole is cut a totally accurate set of measurements can be taken using our piece of string.

A spirit level with built-in protractor is an invaluable tool at this stage. Take a string line from the shaft centre on the ply bracket and run it up to the estimated position on the bottom of the hull where the shaft is expected to pass through. Tape the end of the string in position so that it is tight enough to be straight and then set up the protractor to indicate the angle in relation to the horizontal. Measure the position under the hull and then transfer it inside. Measuring this position from the transom and then remeasuring inside is accurate enough at this stage. Tape another piece of string onto the mark inside the hull and run it up to the engine compartment forward bulkhead (or a ply mock-up if the bulkhead is not yet installed). Use the protractor to set the same angle as the outside string.

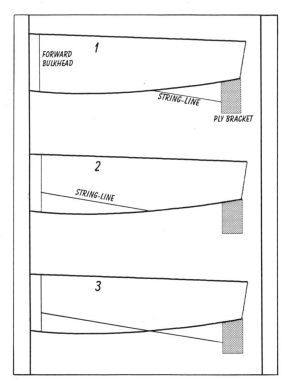

Positioning the propeller shaft. (1) A string line is taken from the temporary bracket to the estimated position where it will pass through the hull. (2) The position is transferred inside and a second string line is set up to confirm that the angle and position is acceptable. (3) A slot is cut in the bottom of the hull and a full-length line is run through from the temporary bracket to the engine compartment forward bulkhead.

Checking the Angles

With the string line set up inside, check the proposed angle of the engine beds in comparison with the water-line. If the vessel has been chocked up correctly the water-line will be horizontal, but in most cases it will be a few degrees off, making it essential to check the engine bed angle directly against the water-line to ensure that the installation is within the engine manufacturer's stated tolerances. If the angle is greater than the manufacturer's tolerances a decision must now be made regarding the feasibility of adjusting the propeller shaft angle or opting for a down-angle gearbox or Aqua-Drive coupling. There is much to be said for using an Aqua-Drive coupling in any installation regardless of alignment problems, as these couplings can greatly reduce vibration when used with very soft engine mounts. Unfortunately they are quite expensive and may be beyond the budget.

The installation angle of the engine with regard to sump clearance below the proposed engine beds must also be checked. The sump clearance decides how far forward on the beds the engine will sit, as the further forward it is mounted the higher it will be above the hull skin. If it all looks feasible recheck everything and prepare to cut the first hole in the bottom

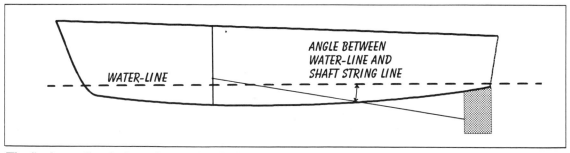

The final propeller shaft angle must be checked against the water-line of the vessel in case the vessel is not chocked up with the water-line horizontal.

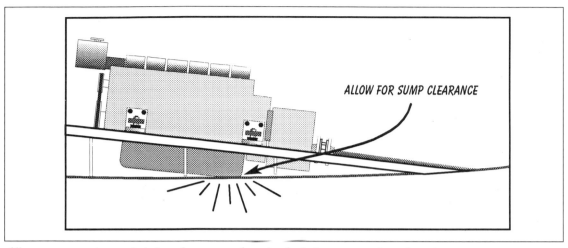

Allowance must be made below the proposed engine beds for sump and gearbox clearance.

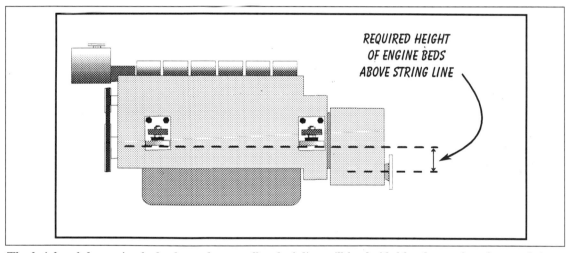

The height of the engine beds above the propeller shaft line will be decided by the gearbox drop and the position of the mounting feet on the engine.

of the boat. If any major problems have arisen, repeat the initial set-up process until all the engine and propeller requirements are met.

A small hole in the bottom of the hull in the position marked can now be cut to allow the string line to pass right through from bracket to bulkhead. It is best to cut a slot to allow the string to run through without touching the hull. This is the line that the shaft and engine

beds will eventually take. The height of the beds above the string line will be decided by the physical size of the engine and the height of the mounting feet in relation to the gearbox output shaft (remember the crucial shaft drop). As far as calculating shaft and engine bed angles is concerned this is about as technical as it gets, yet the results are still sufficiently accurate for the job.

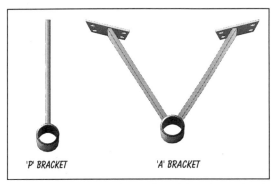

'P' BRACKET   'A' BRACKET

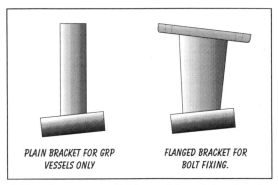

PLAIN BRACKET FOR GRP VESSELS ONLY   FLANGED BRACKET FOR BOLT FIXING.

Different types of shaft bracket. The 'A' bracket is less common on non-commercial vessels.

'P' brackets are available as either plain glass-in types or with mounting flanges for through-bolting.

Shaft Brackets

The next sensible step is to obtain the shaft brackets, either 'off the peg' or made to order. These are either an inverted 'A' section or more commonly a single strut. There are three crucial dimensions to these brackets. The most obvious is the inside diameter of the bearing housing. This must be the correct size to suit the outside diameter of the shaft bearing. The standard shaft bearing for use under water is a water-lubricated rubber bearing with either a phenolic (plastic material very similar to Bakelite) or brass shell. They are available in metric and imperial sizes and it is important to order the correct type. Imperial shaft bearings are available with varying outside diameters to suit each inside (or shaft) diameter. For example, bearings for a 2in shaft are available with outside diameters of $2^5/8$in, $2^3/4$in and 3in. This allows the same 2in shaft to be used in different sized bearing housings. Metric bearings, however, are usually standardized, with one outside diameter for each shaft size. One-off special bearings can also be specified for situations where the standard outside diameter is unsuitable.

The shaft bracket can thus be ordered to suit the outside diameter of the appropriate bearing. The second crucial dimension of the

bracket is the length of the bracket from the hull to the centre of the shaft. The third dimension is the angle of the shaft bearing housing in comparison to the strut. This is important although there is some room for final adjustment when installing the bracket.

Once the shaft bracket is installed this decides the final angle of the engine beds, so it is important to ensure that the angle is satisfactory before final installation. The easiest way to install the shaft bracket in the correct position is to slide it onto the shaft with the bearing fitted and then set up the shaft in the exact required position. Before this can be done the string line slot in the bottom of the hull will need to be opened up to allow the shaft to enter the hull.

Shaft brackets for GRP vessels are often simple straight bronze castings supplied with bearing housings in various sizes to suit all common applications. They are designed to be installed through the hull at the required angle and distance from the hull bottom. They are then bonded into position internally. Being a standard item they are available at reasonable prices.

Shaft brackets designed for a particular vessel or for use on timber craft have cast bases to enable them to be through-bolted into the hull. In this case greater care is needed in

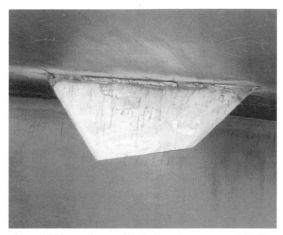

A steel 'P' bracket welded directly to a steel hull.

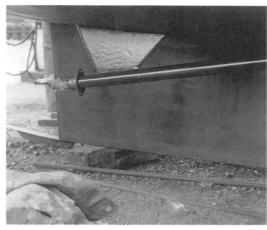

The finished 'P' bracket and steel propeller shaft tube.

A standard, flexibly mounted stuffing box in a GRP vessel.

setting up the bracket as there is less leeway for adjustment than there is with the through hull bonded-in type. Any adjustments to this type of bracket in either angle or distance from the hull can be made using timber wedges or blocks that are bolted into place along with the bracket. In any case, at this stage the shaft bracket should only be temporarily fitted.

For a steel hull the entire bracket can be fabricated from mild steel with the bearing housing made up of simple steel tube of the appropriate size to accommodate the bearing. In this case the bearing and housing can be slipped onto the shaft and the bracket simply cut to shape from steel plate and adjusted until it is a perfect fit. The whole assembly can then be lightly tack-welded together. The rubber bearing must be removed from the steel housing before final welding begins as it will otherwise be melted by the heat from the welding process. However, at this stage the assembly is best left tack welded until the rest of the stern tube assembly has been set up. The same method is used for aluminium hulls using the appropriate grade marine alloy for the bracket and bearing housing.

Installing the Shaft Log

The shaft log can now be installed. This is the fitting that carries the stern tube stuffing box that allows the shaft to pass through the hull and remain watertight. There are more modern alternatives available other than the traditional stuffing box, such as the Deep Sea Seal or the latest oil-lubricated double seal from Halyard Marine. However, they are all installed onto the basic shaft log where the shaft passes through the hull.

The Halyard Marine propeller shaft seal.

The hole in the hull bottom will again need enlarging to accommodate the shaft log. The size of the hole will depend on the type of log used. For GRP craft all that is generally required is a GRP tube bonded through the hull in the correct position. The standard fitting for timber vessels is a plate incorporating a tube for the shaft. The plate is simply bolted inside the hull. Steel and aluminium vessels may only require a tube of the appropriate material to be welded into the hull. In all these cases the actual stuffing box assembly is a flexibly mounted unit that is installed onto the shaft log with hose clips. To ensure that the shaft is still aligned with the 'P' bracket, the log assembly can be slid onto the shaft and set up temporarily using blocks and wedges.

At every stage check that the angle of the shaft still corresponds with the proposed position and angle of the engine beds and that nothing has been inadvertently altered. It is also particularly important with rubber bearings to ensure that the shaft is passing through the bearing in a straight line, as the flexibility of the rubber will allow misalignment during set-up if not checked and corrected.

Once the shaft log and 'P' bracket are set up in their final positions, the angle of the propeller shaft is decided and cannot be adjusted. It is very important therefore to ensure that the alignment is correct before finally bolting, bonding or welding into place. A final word of warning for owners of timber vessels is that as the shaft bracket bolts are

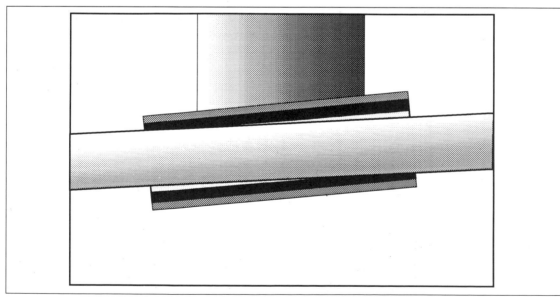

When using a rubber bearing it is easy to set up the shaft and bracket with slight misalignment due to the inherent 'give' in the rubber. This causes vibration and early failure through excessive localized wear.

tightened there is likely to be some crushing of the timber, which may alter the shaft alignment. If this is found to be the case, allowance must be made for the amount of crush before final tightening.

CONSTRUCTING THE ENGINE BEDS

With the worst of the critical calculations completed, the relatively straightforward job of constructing the engine beds can now begin.

There are various methods of designing the beds to suit the engine. I prefer to make drawings of the engine, taking into account the relationship between the various installation components. The position of the gearbox output shaft provides the final position of the engine on the beds in the fore and aft plane. The vertical distance between the rubber mounting feet bottoms and the propeller shaft line gives the height of the beds in relation to the propeller shaft. The depth of the lowest part of the sump below the mounting feet ensures that the engine is in fact far enough forward on the beds to clear the hull skin. Finally, the width apart of the mounting feet provides the distance between the beds.

Another method is to make up a simple ply mock-up of the engine incorporating all the above dimensions. This makes it easier to visualize the final installation for those less used to working with drawings.

How the engine beds are constructed depends largely on the material of the hull. For a steel vessel the normal method is to weld in large steel angle irons and stiffen them with welded cross-members. For timber craft massive baulks of second-hand timber reprieved from building sites are a cost-effective basis for engine beds. These can be cut to shape using a circular saw after first removing any old nails from the timber. With the correct angle ascertained from the string line it is short work to cut the timber to shape, after which the beds can be bolted and glued into position. The same method is also used for GRP vessels, except in this case the beds are bonded into position. Additional cross-members can be added as necessary to suit the engine design and to add to the structural stiffness of the vessel's hull.

Construction for a Repowering Project

Having now looked in some detail at the construction of engine beds in new build vessels, the work of modifying the beds for a repowering project looks quite insignificant. Nevertheless it is just as important to perform an accurate job. For the majority of repowering projects, modifying the engine beds should hopefully consist of little more than widening or narrowing the distance between the beds and raising or lowering the mounting surface to suit the new mounts. If the beds need lowering or the width is to be substantially increased this will involve cutting out the originals and either remodelling them or replacing them completely. If there are extensive differences it is probably better to rebuild from scratch. If the beds are to be raised or the width narrowed then the work is very much simpler. Where there is very little difference between the height of the old and new beds, raising the mounting height may require no more than fitting steel shims beneath the new flexible mounts.

Even when there is a significant increase in height the work is still straightforward. If the beds are timber or GRP-bonded timber then raising them is simply a matter of adding additional timbers to the top face to raise them to the required height. For steel beds it is possible to make up boxes that are welded onto the original beds corresponding with the position of the new engine's mounts. Narrowing the beds is simply a matter of

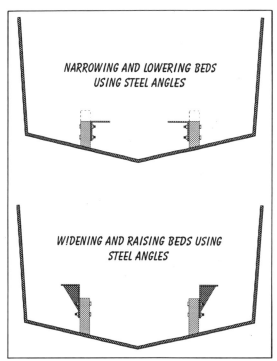

Original engine beds can usually be modified for both height and width using welded steel angle irons. These can be either welded or bolted to the original beds depending on the original material.

accept the weight of the engine and to transmit the thrust of the propeller but they do not have to be constructed to the exacting requirements of the engine. Instead, the needs of the engine are accommodated by the frame. When repowering, this is often an easier option than totally rebuilding the engine beds. It depends how different the old and new engines are. The frame is the secondary engine bed that will eventually be bolted or welded onto the primary engine bed built into the boat.

The frame in its most basic form consists of steel angle irons running along each side of the engine onto which the engine mounting feet will be bolted. The frame must be strong enough to support the weight of the engine and accept the thrust of the propeller once installed. For engines with a capacity of up to about ten litres, 4in by 4in (100mm x 100mm) angle irons are strong enough. Cross-members welded between the two outer angles complete the frame while webs and stiffeners are added as required. During construction, allowance must be made for the sump and the gearbox

bolting new timbers between the inner faces of timber or GRP-bonded beds, or again welding boxes or angle irons onto steel beds. In all cases the installation angle must be borne in mind and whether or not a universal joint coupling or down-angle gearbox is to be used.

THE FRAME

Once the basic engine beds are in place and at the correct angle many people find it easier to construct an engine mounting frame away from the boat. The basic full-strength engine beds must be installed within the boat to

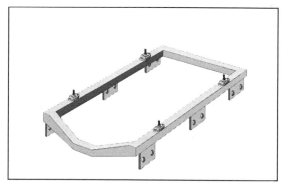

An engine mounting frame can be as simple or elaborate as required as long as it (and the primary engine beds) are sufficiently strong for the weight and thrust of the engine.

output shaft so that when the frame is complete the engine sits on it without any parts fouling the frame.

If the position of the gearbox output shaft is marked on the frame prior to its installation, it will act as a guide to the final position of the frame (and therefore the engine) once installed. As the frame is a fraction of the weight of the engine it can easily be positioned accurately onto the primary engine beds to allow the fixing flanges to be made up and welded onto the frame prior to engine installation. This type of frame can usefully be used for all types of boat construction as the final fastening into place can be by either welding or bolting.

When working with fibre-glass materials in the confined space of an engine compartment it is important to make proper preparations for ventilating the area before commencing work. Industrial extractor fans can be hired from your local plant hire shop and are well worth the small cost involved. A plentiful supply of cheap plastic gloves to protect hands from the catalysed resin are another essential. I do not intend to cover the process of working with fibre-glass as there are many books available on the subject. Besides, I am sure anyone contemplating repowering a GRP vessel will already have hands-on experience of working with fibre-glass.

COUPLINGS

In all cases it is important to use a flexible coupling between the gearbox output shaft and the propeller shaft coupling. This helps to prevent vibrations being transmitted down the shaft and into the vessel. It also takes some of the shock out of the propeller hitting underwater obstructions, and in the worst case acts as the weak link to protect the gearbox from damage in the event of severe propeller impact. One thing the standard flexible cou-

An R & D Marine flexible propeller shaft coupling

pling does not do is to relieve the owner of the task of aligning the gearbox and propeller shaft couplings accurately. Typically the acceptable radial alignment of these coupling faces is less than 0.005in, and we will be covering the methods of accurate shaft alignment in Chapter 8.

Where a non-aligned shaft installation is required but a down-angle gearbox is not desired, possibly because the original gearbox is being used for the new installation, then a universal joint coupling must be used. The Aqua-Drive coupling from Halyard Marine is very popular because of its relative ease of installation and time-proven reliability. As already mentioned these couplings are now quite often used for aligned as well as non-aligned installations. The reason for this is that they accept the shaft thrust rather than letting it be passed onto the gearbox as with a standard installation. This prevents vibrations being transmitted down the shaft and into the hull and also allows the use of softer engine mounts, thus further reducing vibration.

As the coupling incorporates a heavy-duty thrust bearing to accept the thrust of the propeller it is important that it is strongly mounted. The usual method is to fabricate a steel cross-member that is either bolted or welded between the engine beds at the inboard end of the propeller shaft. This must be strong enough to transmit the thrust of the propeller to the boat without any movement or give. Once the thrust-bearing carrier is installed it is then easy to couple the universal joint shaft to the gearbox output shaft. The only point to check is that the two universal joints in the system are both at the same angle and that in a non-aligned installation the angle between shaft and engine does not exceed the recommended maximum for the universal joint coupling.

ACCESS

This is a good time to think about access for lifting the old engine out and the new engine in. If the engine is mounted below the cockpit floor with easy access from above with the hatches removed there will be few problems. However, if the engine is located below the wheelhouse floor there is the problem of access for the crane hoist.

In the long term the best option is to cut an access hatch in the roof over the engine bay. The hatch itself should be flush fitting and undetected as the seams are filled and faired off before deck paint (or other deck covering) is applied over the entire surface. As it will hopefully only be used once in the life of the boat there is no need to have it ready for instant access. When it needs to be opened all that is required is that the filler is dug out, the securing bolts removed and the entire section prised out. This gives direct access for a crane hoist into the engine compartment making it possible to lift the old engine out and the new one in with a direct lift.

This may seem a drastic step to take but it is almost certainly better to accept the extra work involved with cutting an access hatch into the wheelhouse roof than it is to try and manhandle engines in and out through the doors. I have tried both methods and the latter tends to cause more damage and injury than the former. It also means that should the engine ever have to come for service or repair the access hatch is there, ready to be opened once again. Obviously once the hatch is cut it is important to stiffen the entire roof to retain the original strength once it is refitted, but this is not difficult and more than compensated for by the peace of mind of knowing that the engine is easily accessible should the need arise for repair. This type of hatch is standard on many larger vessels and some of the better-quality smaller models also have them installed.

PLANNING CHECKLIST

Item to be Checked	
Performance required. Maximum and cruising speed?	Max.: Cruise:
Is vessel's design capable of providing the above performance?	Y/N
Power required to achieve above performance?	— bhp — kW
Is vessel's hull capable of handling the above power?	Check with builder:
Propeller shaft diameter is correct for the torque produced?	Check with Prop supplier:
Propeller shaft diameter required for the torque produced?	— in — mm
Upsize the entire stern gear to correct above?	Y/N
Specify high-strength alloy shaft as alternative to above?	Y/N
Warranties offered by different engine suppliers compared?	Y/N
Suitable gearbox/es to handle the power of the engine/s selected. (See below also)	Make and type.
Gearboxes selected with capacity for engine's power?	Y/N
Gearbox/es can run continuously in either direction for contra-rotation in twin engine installations?	Y/N
For twin engines, gearboxes selected with identical forward and reverse ratios?	Y/N
Duty cycle for chosen engine is correct for vessel's proposed operation?	Duty cycle type:
Room in the engine compartment to fit the engine/s?	Y/N
Sufficient ventilation within the engine compartment for the engine's combustion and cooling needs?	Required cross-section of engine comp. vents:
Modifications required within the vessel are feasible?	Y/N
Sufficient propeller tip clearance for larger propellers to suit new engine?	Required prop diameter: Tip clearance:
Suitable location for performing the work?	Place:
Lifting equipment available?	Y/N

PREPARING THE BOAT FOR THE ENGINE

5

The preparations required to install an engine into a boat obviously vary considerably between different makes and types of boat. Even boats of the same make and type will probably have evolved over the years as their owners made major or minor alterations. The initial planning will indicate what is required in each individual case so this section is devoted to recounting my own preparations.

Having gone through the entire planning stage of calculating how much power I could safely and usefully install within *Pershilla*'s hull, I then selected the engine and gearbox for the job and ascertained that a high strength alloy shaft was capable of taking the power, removing the need to cut out and replace the entire stern gear. For me this was the main deciding factor on how much power I could install as my budget would not stretch to rebuilding the entire engine compartment and replacing the stern gear. But at this stage I knew that all the research and planning had been worth while as I was about to begin the job for real with a clear idea of exactly what was involved and how much it would cost.

The first part of the job was to recheck all my calculations, this time working to the close tolerances provided by the fully dimensioned engine drawing. This was supplied by Cummins together with an extremely comprehensive installation manual. It was good to confirm that the engine and gearbox would actually fit *Pershilla*'s engine compartment without any further changes being required other than those originally planned for during the early stages. Other than this I did not begin any real preparation, beyond lifting out the Bedford, until the new engine and gearbox were delivered.

REMOVING THE OLD ENGINE

A couple of years previously I had converted *Pershilla* from her standard De-Groot layout with the upper helm on the deck aft of the wheelhouse to fly-bridge configuration. In the process of doing this I had a removable, flush-fitting hatch built into the fly-bridge aluminium floor over the engine compartment. This was included to make engine removal and replacement very much easier when the time came, and it immediately proved its worth when we lifted out the Bedford. I well remember the problems when the Bedford was last removed for a rebuild in 1991. It had to be hauled up to floor level using a hoist shackled to the wheelhouse roof (one of the advantages of steel construction). As it weighed close to a ton with the gearbox attached this was no mean feat. Once it was chocked up on the

Pershilla in original form with helm aft of wheelhouse.

The later modified Pershilla with fly-bridge.

Propeller shaft disconnected prior to hoisting out the old Bedford.

wheelhouse floor it then had to be stripped down to the bare block so that it could be manhandled bit by bit out of the wheelhouse ready to be taken down to the reconditioner. It was subsequently rebuilt in the wheelhouse and reinstalled in the reverse manner.

Having replaced the steel roof with an aluminium fabrication there was no possibility of using a hoist from the roof for lifting purposes. This was one reason for installing the hatch. When we lifted out the Bedford prior to fitting the Cummins all I had to do was unbolt the hatch and pass the hook of the crane hoist down to the strops already lashed around the

The Bedford being removed from Pershilla for the last time.

The roof hatch designed into the fly-bridge made engine changing easy.

block. The propeller shaft was uncoupled and the engine mounting bolts removed. The fuel, water, exhaust and electrical connections were disconnected and she was ready for lifting.

As the engine and gearbox was longer than the 40in (100cm) of the hatch we had to experiment with the lifting angle until we were able to lift it nose high straight out of the engine compartment, through the roof and down onto the waiting chocks alongside. Overall the job took less than an hour. The previous removal had taken a day and a half. I am emphasizing this aspect of the work to stress the ease that a roof hatch offers for engine maintenance purposes.

PREPARING THE NEW ENGINE AT THE FACTORY

With the Bedford out of the boat I removed the Bosch alternator to retain for use on the Cummins. As this is a high output alternator

The Bedford sitting on chocks waiting for the alternator to be removed.

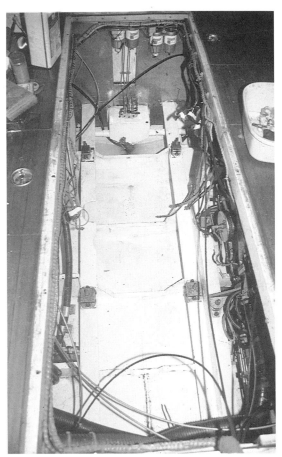

Meanwhile at the Cummins factory . . . fitting the damper drive plate.

The engine compartment with the Bedford removed and awaiting preparation for the Cummins.

Swinging the gearbox into position for alignment with the drive plate.

modified for use with an Adverc external regulator I wanted to keep it as part of the system. Cummins suggested I send it to them for installing onto the engine at the factory in line with their approved fitting procedure. Naturally I was quite happy to offload another job.

The process of installing the gearbox onto the engine is not unduly complicated, but the weight of the gearbox makes it difficult to line up with the splines of the drive plate without some form of lifting tackle to take the weight during the alignment process. The damper

drive plate was first installed onto the engine flywheel. This was followed by the gearbox, which at the factory was supported by a custom-built hoist. The charge air transfer tube between the turbo-charger and the after-cooler was then fitted, followed by the oil-cooler pipework.

Next the crankshaft end float was checked to ensure that the gearbox was not applying pressure to the crankshaft. Once this reading was found to be satisfactory the job was completed by finally tightening all the securing bolts around the gearbox housing.

Refitting the turbo-charger charge air transfer pipe.

Checking the crankshaft end float.

Reconnecting the oil cooler pipes.

Preparing the engine for the alternator mounting bracket.

The Bosch alternator with Adverc modifications was fitted.

Fitting the drive belt and checking for alignment.

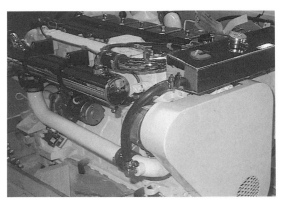

The belt guard installed.

The engine complete and ready for shipping to Gillingham.

The alternator mounting bracket was fitted at the front of the engine together with the Bosch alternator. The driver belt was threaded over the pulleys while the self-adjusting belt tensioner was held out of the way using a $^3/_8$in square drive ratchet. Once the belt was correctly in place and the alignment of the alternator pulley checked, the cover plate was reinstalled and the engine was ready for shipping out to Gillingham.

The original propeller was removed prior to sliding the old stainless steel shaft out of the tube via the hole in the rudder blade. The old Cutless bearing could now be removed before installing a new one. Having been in place for several years this was very firmly stuck in place and had no intention of coming out easily. However, as it was a phenolic-bodied rubber bearing, it could be cut with woodworking tools, and a sharp chisel soon had the old bearing out in several shattered pieces. Installation of the new rubber bearing was simply a matter of sliding it into position and screwing on the tube end cover.

PREPARING THE ENGINE COMPARTMENT

Once the new engine arrived with gearbox and alternator duly mounted I began making the detailed drawings of the engine mount positions in relation to the gearbox output flange to decide how high or low the engine was to be mounted in relation to the propeller shaft. On the Bedford the bases of the flexible engine mounts were almost at the same level as the shaft so the engine beds were originally installed about $^1/_4$in (6mm) below the centre-line of the shaft. On the Cummins the flexible mounts' bases were approximately 4in (100mm) above the centre-line of the shaft. This meant building up the original beds by $3^1/_2$in (90mm) to accommodate this difference in height. The engine itself was at the same

The Cummins arrives at Gillingham on a pallet.

height as the Bedford in relation to the gearbox flange. The only difference was the position of the mounting feet on the engine block. The mounts were also slightly nearer the centre-line than on the Bedford so the new beds had to be narrower. As the local strength of steel is inherently great, I fabricated four boxes from $^{3}/_{8}$in steel plate purchased from a scrapyard for a few pence!

Before I could weld the raised engine bed boxes into position I had to carefully measure the position of the mounting feet in relation to the gearbox output flange. But before I could do this the new propeller shaft had to be installed to provide the fore and aft position of the engine on the beds. The propeller shaft was slid up the tube and set up roughly in the correct position. The two halves of the Deep Sea Shaft Seal were slipped over the shaft for

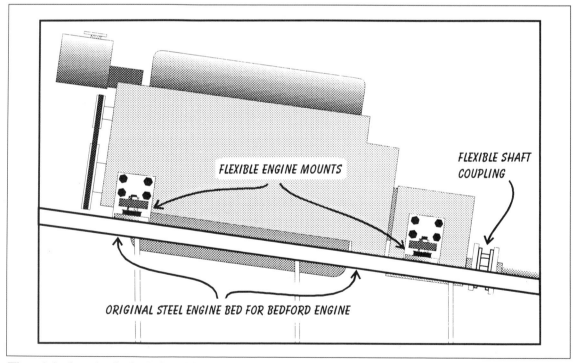

The original engine beds designed for the Bedford at the correct height for the engine mounting feet in relation to the propeller shaft.

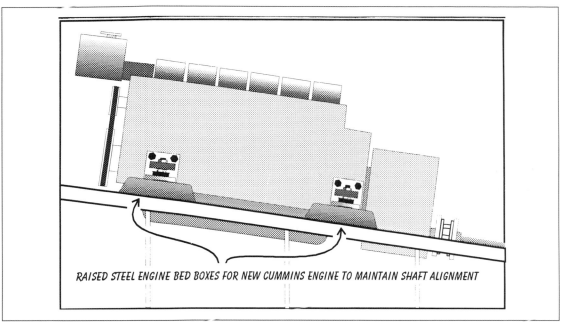

RAISED STEEL ENGINE BED BOXES FOR NEW CUMMINS ENGINE TO MAINTAIN SHAFT ALIGNMENT

The engine bed boxes had to be raised for the Cummins to maintain the correct height for the propeller shaft. The Cummins engine is in fact at the same height as the Bedford, it is the position of the engine mounting feet on the block that is different.

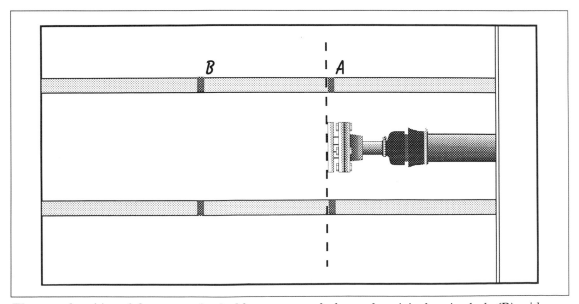

The central position of the new engine bed boxes was marked onto the original engine beds (B) with regard to the position of the inboard end of the propeller shaft and flexible coupling (A).

Engine bed boxes welded into position and painted.

Detail of the starboard floor support, which was cut out, moved back 2in (50mm) and rewelded into position.

fitting later, followed by the shaft half-coupling, which was secured with a steel-bodied Nyloc self-locking nut smothered in waterproof grease. The R & D flexible coupling was also temporarily fitted to enable the accurate calculation of the eventual position of the gearbox coupling. The shaft was then slid into its correct position, allowing for the required clearance between the propeller and the rudder. The engine beds were marked in line with the coupling face and the final positions of the engine mounting feet were measured from these marks. The positions of the engine mounting feet were then marked onto the beds and the raised engine bed boxes were welded permanently into place at the four marks.

On a GRP or wooden vessel the new beds would normally run the full length of the old beds and be either bolted or bonded into position. This saves the need to measure the fore and aft position of the feet accurately at this stage as the engine position can be altered by sliding it fore and aft to suit the propeller shaft coupling once roughly in position.

As we have already seen, although the Cummins engine mounts were closer together than those of the Bedford, the rest of the equipment on the Cummins made it significantly wider overall. I now commenced the task of cutting out the wheelhouse floor supports and moving them outwards. As they were both steel angle irons I cut them out using a 4½in angle grinder and metal cutting disc. Heavy dust sheets were used to catch the filings as the proximity of the wing engine precluded using gas cutting gear.

The starboard support was cut out in its entirety and moved outwards 2in (50mm), where it was welded into its new position. The port support could not be moved completely owing to the proximity of the battery box, so instead I cut out a 1in (25mm) section,

The entire engine compartment, converted, freshly painted throughout and ready for the new engine.

vessel and certainly a lot cleaner, but it is important to ensure that the rebuilt supports have the same strength as the originals.

I then set about checking and rechecking all the dimensions until paranoia set in and I was finally satisfied that the engine compartment was ready to accept the new Cummins.

PREPARING FOR THE NEW EXHAUST

With the Bedford out of the way and the engine compartment freshly painted I removed the old Vetus water-lock silencer and the flexible exhaust hoses. The home-made steel watertight bulkhead fitting that took the

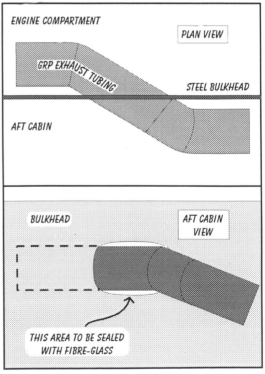

The 'dog-leg' GRP exhaust elbows to allow a smooth gas flow through the steel bulkhead and provide a sealed, watertight fitting.

reversed it and welded it onto the back of the remainder of the support, reinforcing it with small in-fill plates at the top and bottom. Once again the inherent strength of steel made the job quick and easy, if not very clean. The final job was to clean out all the swarf and grindings and paint the entire bilge area with three coats of International Interprotect epoxy. This included the engine beds, athwartship supports and all the other places it is impossible to reach when the engine is in place.

For timber or GRP vessels the cutting out of floor supports to make way for the engine is probably more straightforward than on a steel exhaust through the aft bulkhead was unbolted and discarded. On examining this I was surprised at how little corrosion there was after seven years of service in salt water. It was of no further use so was bundled with the rest of the exhaust pipework for sale at the next boat jumble.

Taking advantage of the space in the engine compartment to move around with comparative ease, I enlarged the opening in the bulkhead to accept the new 6in exhaust. This time, rather than fabricating a new steel fitting I decided to use modified fibre-glass elbows as supplied by Halyard Marine for use with their exhaust hose. Two 45-degree elbows were bonded together in a dog-leg fashion to allow the exhaust to run smoothly through the bulkhead with the minimum of disruption to the aft cabin furniture. The plan was to bond them to the steel bulkhead once the exhaust hoses were fitted to retain the watertight integrity of the bulkhead.

Once through the bulkhead the exhaust runs out to the starboard side of the hull and passes a four-drawer chest built into the forward lower bulkhead of the aft cabin. The original 3in exhaust allowed enough clearance to open all four drawers but with the 6in tube it looked as though I would have to sacrifice at least one drawer in the chest.

At the transom there were originally separate 3in and 2in exhaust outlets mounted side by side – one for the Bedford, the other for the BMC wing engine. The difference in size had not been great and they matched fairly well. However, the difference between a 6in and a 2in exhaust was obviously so different that I decided to design a single fitting to accommodate both outlets.

My original idea had been a single 6in outlet with the 2in wing exhaust feeding into the main tubing via a 'Y' piece. However, Halyard Marine advised against this because there was a risk of exhaust water being forced into the wing engine when it was not running owing to the pressure of the water and gases produced with the Cummins under power. The final design of the combined 6in and 2in transom fitting was fabricated from stainless steel by D. W. Davies of Canvey Island and proved to be both smart and practical. Fitting it involved cutting an access hatch in the centre of the headboard of the bed and removing a stiffening panel behind to allow the exhaust hose to run up to the fitting. Obviously I also had to cut an enlarged hole in the transom to accept the new fitting.

Having fixed the position of the exhaust hose through the bulkhead where it entered the aft cabin and its exit through the transom, all I then had to do was make room for it behind the cabin furniture with the minimum of harm. In the event it was not as problematical as I had expected and only required careful enlarging of the original openings where the exhaust passed behind the four-drawer cabinet, behind the bedside cabinet and beneath the bed.

6

INSTALLING THE NEW ENGINE

After all the preparation and planning that had gone into the project so far it was good to be starting the actual installation work.

Safety must always be a major consideration when working in an industrial environment. Whether the work is being performed in the garden at home or within the confines of a boatyard, the job is still very much an industrial project with all the inherent risks involved. An engine weighing in at around a ton needs care when handling. It is not only the avoidance of injury that must be borne in mind but also the cost of replacing anything that becomes damaged. These are two very good reasons for using a crane for all lifting work on big engines. I had used the services of the Gillingham Marina crane to lift out the Bedford a couple of weeks prior to beginning the installation, and as I had prepared everything in advance the total cost of lifting out the engine was half an hour's labour.

LIFTING IN THE ENGINE

Preparation for lifting the Cummins in consisted of removing various parts from the starboard side of the engine. The engine itself is over 30in (75cm) wide while the deck aperture is 24in (60cm). By removing the heat exchanger, the exhaust water injection elbow

from the turbo-charger, the freshwater cooling pipe between the block and the heat exchanger and the oil filter, the width was reduced to near the required 24in. When it is only isolated parts that are extending out farther than the required width, once the engine is hanging in the slings it can usually be twisted and tilted around to avoid these parts. Using heavy nylon ropes the engine was slung nose up and carefully hoisted into the air. The nose-up attitude effectively shortened the length of the engine to allow it to pass through the 40in (100cm) long access hatch in the roof.

Once over the side of the fly-bridge it was lowered towards the open access hatch. Blankets had been arranged all round the

Removing Cummins parts prior to lifting in.

Carefully preparing the lashings for the lift.

Stuck on a bracket while passing through the roof.

The engine was lifted nose-up onto the fly-bridge to allow it to fit through the roof hatch.

Once the bracket was moved the engine slid neatly through the hatch.

hatch opening to try to avoid damage to the engine or the hatch surround. The gearbox end of the engine passed through the hatch but was then stopped by a relay bracket bolted to the starter motor mounting. This was fastened with one of only three Torx header bolts on the engine. These are the multi-pointed bolt heads now being used on some cars but were still so rare that no one in the yard had a suitable socket set. It was too tight to slacken with a vice grip or pipe wrench but after some discussion, Graham, our photographer, grabbed a large adjustable spanner and using it as a lever moved the bracket out of the way by twisting it in the direction that would unscrew the bolt. This approach worked as the

bolt moved round with the bracket and no damage was done. I subsequently mentioned this bolt type anomaly to Cummins UK who could come up with no logical reason why Torx head bolts were used on this one isolated section.

With the bracket out of the way the engine easily passed through the roof and down into the wheelhouse. We then moved inside and continued lowering the engine between the floor supports and onto the waiting beds. Despite several attempts to get it sitting straight on the beds, the engine continually tilted to one side or the other. This was because of the acute nose-up angle at which it was still slung. We then hoisted it back up to

Fruitlessly lowering the engine onto the beds while still nose-up.

Cutting out the edge of the oversized engine bed box with the engine chocked-up above.

The engine finally sitting in place accompanied by sighs of relief all round!

floor level and chocked it up on blocks to enable the sling to be refitted to allow the engine to hang level. It was then lowered into position where it sat almost perfectly.

I say 'almost' because the new rear bed boxes were too close together to allow the flywheel housing to fit between them. Despite all my careful measurements I had managed to miss one crucial dimension, which meant that the rear engine bed boxes were each a 1/4in (6mm) too wide. The engine now had to be hoisted again and chocked up at floor level while I got underneath with the grinder and cut 1/2in (12mm) off the inside edge of both rear bed boxes. This was followed by a thorough clean-up with the dust pan, brush and vacuum cleaner to remove all the metal grinding dust from what had been a pristine engine compartment. The engine was again lowered into position and this time it sat down squarely on the new beds.

As soon as the engine was sitting in place another minor problem revealed itself. There was insufficient access around the rear engine feet to drill the holes in the new engine bed boxes for securing the flexible mounts to the beds. By the time this was noticed, the roof hatch and head-lining had been reinstalled to

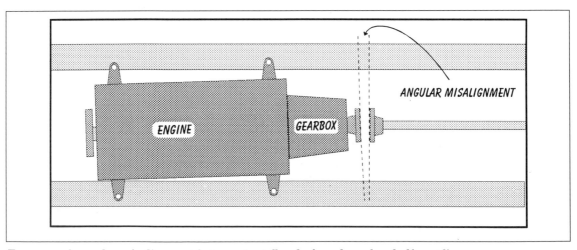

Exaggerated angular misalignment between propeller shaft and gearbox half-couplings.

enable the piles of fibre-glass loft insulation to be refitted. This made it impossible to use the boat-hoist crane to lift the engine unless the head-lining and roof were removed again. Not wishing to be covered in fibre-glass loft insulation for a third time I decided to set up two stacks of heavy wooden blocks on the wheelhouse floor each side of the engine access hatch, and place scaffold poles across the two so that a portable chain hoist could be used to lift the rear of the engine and thus provide the necessary room for drilling the holes.

ALIGNING THE ENGINE

Before this could be done the position of the new propeller shaft and half-coupling had to be checked to enable the engine to be aligned with it. The position of the engine fixing bolt holes decides the final athwartship position of the engine and it is therefore vital to get the engine aligned with the shaft coupling before drilling the holes. The flexible engine mounts have slotted holes to allow a small amount of athwartship movement for final alignment but this is not sufficient to correct large errors: it is important to get the initial alignment as near perfect as possible.

With the portable hoist set up on blocks, initial engine and shaft alignment could begin. The engine was roughly aligned with the shaft by physically moving it across the beds to align the coupling faces. At this stage a lot of fiddling about can ensue as the engine is moved around to get the initial angular and linear alignment. Angular alignment refers to the mating of the coupling faces to ensure that when they are bolted together they are perfectly flush fitting. If there is any angular misalignment the shaft will run with a permanent twist, causing vibration and stress on the shaft, bearings and gearbox, leading in turn to shorter component life. The same applies to linear alignment. If the couplings are bolted up with the engine and shaft out of alignment the same stresses will again be set up.

With a rope slung under the engine between the rear of the block and the flywheel housing the weight was taken on the hoist. The engine could then be slid back and forth across the beds until initial alignment was achieved between the gearbox and shaft couplings. Engine height in relation to the shaft is not a critical factor at this stage so I could now

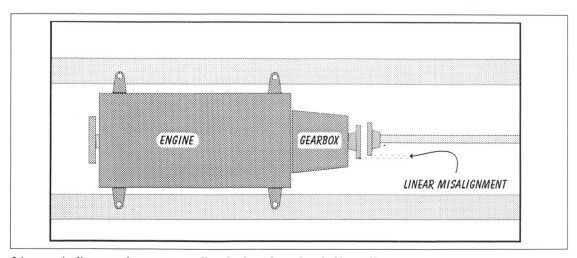

Linear misalignment between propeller shaft and gearbox half-couplings.

mark the position of the engine mount fixing holes through the mount bases with an indelible marker pen.

The front mount holes were accessible to the electric drill without lifting the engine so I first drilled one hole for each of the front mounts by passing the drill bit through the mounting flange. I was then able to bolt the front mounts temporarily to the beds to prevent the engine slipping once the rear was lifted to provide access for drilling the rear mount holes.

The rear of the engine was then lifted squarely until there was sufficient room for the drill to be lined up with the marks on the beds. Although I was using 12mm bolts for holding the engine down I drilled the fixing holes to

13mm. This provided a little extra clearance in the holes to allow for the inaccuracies of drilling with a hand-held electric drill in a confined space. The slight slack in the bolt holes is not sufficient to cause any loss of strength but makes assembly much easier.

Aligning the Gearbox Coupling and Shaft

With the holes drilled and the fixing bolts loosely fitted the final alignment of the gearbox coupling and shaft could commence. The final alignment is crucial to the success of the whole project and must be accurately performed. Although it requires care it is no more complicated than the initial alignment

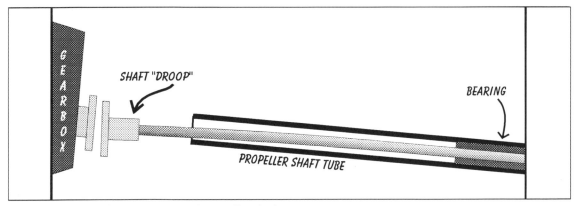

Shaft 'droop' on a long unsupported propeller shaft.

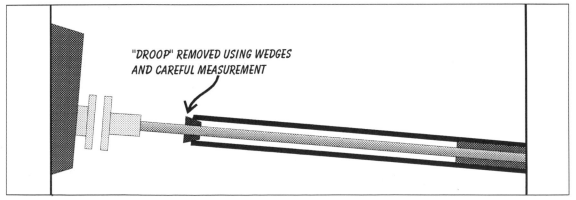

'Droop' removed temporarily with wedges prior to final engine alignment.

and only requires patience and precise measurement. The alignment process should be carried out without the flexible coupling that will eventually fit between the gearbox and shaft to ensure that the steel faces of the half-couplings align perfectly before the less precise rubber or plastic flexible coupling is introduced.

The first step is to ensure there is no 'droop' in the shaft between the last bearing and the coupling end of the shaft. This is only necessary when the shaft is long and there is a large unsupported length of shaft between the last bearing and the coupling, as is the case with *Pershilla*. The spacing between the shaft and tube was measured top and bottom, left and right, and the shaft supported with wedges until the droop was removed.

The gearbox half-coupling was now ready for aligning with the shaft half-coupling. These couplings are machined with a matching spigot and aperture to ensure they mate perfectly but to further ensure that they are

properly aligned the mating faces must be kept apart until the alignment process is finished. It is possible (and quite easy) to let the two mating faces slip together while they are still misaligned. Although they will then appear to be in alignment the shaft may be forced into a slight curve that is invisible to the naked eye. The result will be shaft whip, vibration and early bearing failure. To ensure that this does not happen, the two mating faces must be aligned with the faces parted.

Athwartship and Vertical Alignment

Athwartship alignment is achieved by moving the engine and its mounts either left or right across the boat (using the transverse slotted bolt holes in the mounts), while vertical alignment is achieved using the adjusting nuts on the flexible mounts. However, it is recommended that when using these adjusters the nuts should be as near to the bottom of the thread as possible to prevent excessive angular movement of the threaded studs under prop

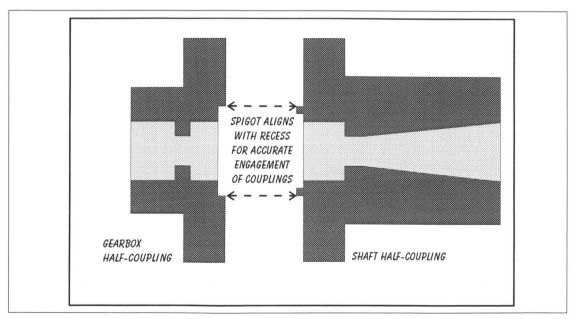

Half-coupling mating faces align with a central spigot. It is essential to keep these faces apart until initial alignment is complete.

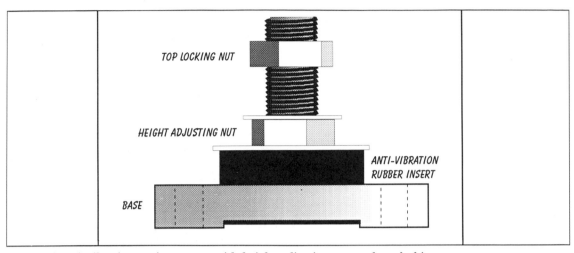

A typical anti-vibration engine mount with height adjusting nut and top locking nut.

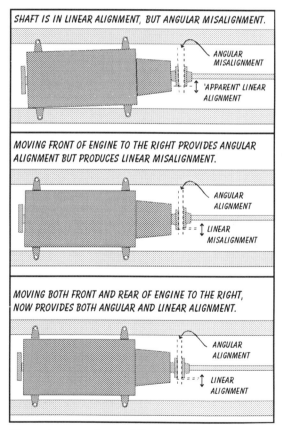

Removing angular and linear shaft misalignment.

shaft thrust. This makes it important to ensure that there is very little vertical misalignment before final adjustments are made. With the Cummins I was only able to get the couplings into alignment with the adjusting nuts right at the top of the threads, making it impossible to fit the top lock nut and providing far too much scope for angular movement. Yet another small miscalculation despite all the checking and rechecking!

The mounts ideally needed raising by $^3/_4$in to allow the adjusting nuts to sit near the bottom of the threads. Steel packing shims were obviously the easiest and cheapest way to raise the flexible mounts. These were gas cut from pieces of scrap $^1/_2$in and $^1/_4$in plate, cleaned up with the angle grinder and painted with several coats of International Interprotect epoxy for steel. Using the hoist and blocks to lift the engine, first the front and then the rear shims were placed under the flexible mounts and the alignment process began again.

Linear and Angular Alignment
Linear and initial angular alignment must be checked at the same time because one affects

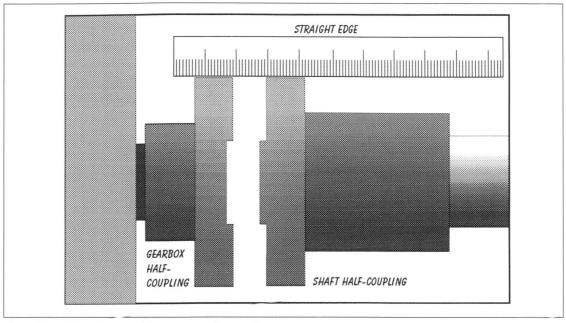

STRAIGHT EDGE

GEARBOX
HALF-
COUPLING

SHAFT HALF-COUPLING

A steel straight-edge provides accurate linear alignment.

the other. Moving the back of the engine to bring the couplings into linear alignment generally means that the front will also need moving to maintain the angular alignment. By only moving the back an angular misalignment is introduced that must be checked and removed. The subsequent moving of the front of the engine then introduces another linear misalignment at the coupling. The process must be repeated until the couplings are in both linear and angular alignment. A steel straight-edge laid along the edge of both coupling flanges shows linear alignment. Measuring the gap between the couplings provides initial angular alignment.

Accurate linear alignment must be completed at this stage – once the couplings are bolted together it is impossible to check this aspect because of the flexibility of the propeller shaft, which will always appear to be aligned when subsequently bolted up to the gearbox coupling.

Installing the Flexible Coupling

With the couplings approximately aligned the shaft was slid back to allow the flexible coupling to be installed between the two

Shaft couplings bolted together with R & D flexible coupling between. Note the wire earthing bridge, which ensures that the shaft and propeller are protected by the hull's anode system.

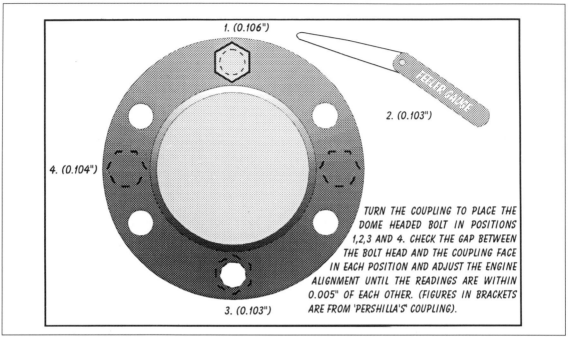

1. (0.106")

2. (0.103")

4. (0.104")

TURN THE COUPLING TO PLACE THE DOME HEADED BOLT IN POSITIONS 1,2,3 AND 4. CHECK THE GAP BETWEEN THE BOLT HEAD AND THE COUPLING FACE IN EACH POSITION AND ADJUST THE ENGINE ALIGNMENT UNTIL THE READINGS ARE WITHIN 0.005" OF EACH OTHER. (FIGURES IN BRACKETS ARE FROM 'PERSHILLA'S' COUPLING).

3. (0.103")

Final accurate shaft alignment is performed using a feeler gauge.

half-couplings. In this case a coupling from R & D Marine was used to provide the shock and vibration protection. There are six bolts to each half-coupling, one of which has a domed head to permit very accurate final angular alignment of the couplings.

The procedure I used was to turn the shaft until the domed head was at the 12 o'clock position. The gap between the domed head and coupling face was then measured using feeler gauges. I made a note of the measurement and turned the shaft so that the domed head was at the 6 o'clock position. Again I measured the gap and made a note of the reading. I used the same procedure to measure the 3 o'clock and 9 o'clock positions: these last two should already read the same if the initial lining-up was accurate.

Final Adjustments

The adjusting nuts on the flexible feet were then used to adjust the angle of the engine in conjunction with the shaft. Any athwartship angular misalignment had then to be removed by again moving the engine left or right by very small amounts. This was achieved by slackening the holding-down bolts and lightly tapping the mounts in the required direction. (This will usually be the front mounts, as these have the greatest effect on angular alignment. Tap the port mount and then tap the starboard mount the same number of times. This will result in the very small movements required to adjust the coupling alignment by a few thousands of an inch each time.)

When the difference between the measured

gap at each of the four positions was less than five-thousandths of an inch, the engine and shaft were satisfactorily aligned and the lock nuts on the mounts and mount securing bolts could finally be tightened. The Deep Sea Seal was then refitted.

For wooden and GRP vessels it is essential to perform the final alignment when the vessel is afloat because of the inherent flexibility of the hull. From previous experience I knew that in *Pershilla*'s case, like most relatively small steel vessels, there is no hull flex, thanks to the enormous strength of their egg-box-like structures. Despite this the alignment was rechecked once *Pershilla* was afloat just for peace of mind.

REFITTING THE EXTERNAL PARTS

With the engine accurately aligned it was time to refit the parts that had been removed to allow the engine to pass through the roof hatch. This was a straightforward procedure with only one point worth mentioning, concerning the oil filter. Good maintenance practice states that when an oil and filter change is due, the filter body should be filled with oil to prevent a period of dry running before the filter fills from the sump after start up. This was also mentioned in the Cummins maintenance manual and it was therefore pleasing to find that when I removed the filter

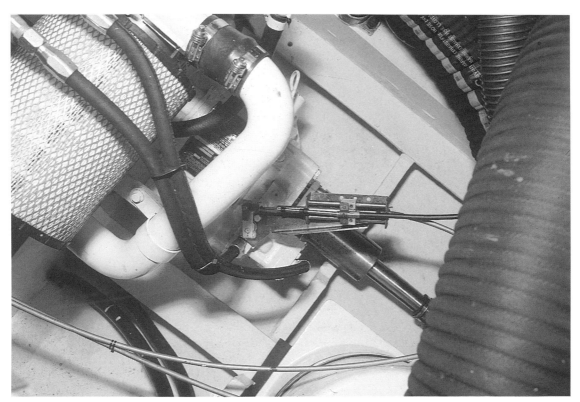

Gear cables connected into a dual station unit mounted on the Twin Disc cable bracket.

A tight fit between the Cummins water injection elbow and the wing engine air filter.

on this new engine to allow clearance through the roof, it was indeed already filled with oil.

The gear and throttle cables were connected using the brackets supplied by Cummins and Twin Disc, but slightly modified to accept the standard dual-station converter units that had previously been used on the Bedford.

Now that the engine was finally sitting in position and bolted down in alignment with the shaft, the heavy work was complete. The clearance between the air filter on the wing engine and the exhaust water injection elbow on the Cummins was always going to be tight and I had already worked out a plan to move the filter out of the way if necessary. However, with the injection elbow refitted there was about 2in (5cm) between the two parts, making modification unnecessary.

THE FUEL SYSTEM

7

Installation of a new engine is a good time to consider the design of the fuel system. There is little point in installing a brand new engine only to compromise its reliability with an inefficient and dirty fuel system. At the very least the tank should be thoroughly cleaned out to remove all traces of sediment and water. When you consider that the majority of call-outs to power boats by lifeboats are due to fuel-related problems the need for a clean fuel system becomes self-evident. Simply replacing the fuel filters on an annual basis is not enough to ensure reliability. The tanks must be clean if the filters are not to be overwhelmed

with dirt and water whenever they get stirred up in choppy weather.

The usual recommendation for twin engines is to have separate fuel tanks, with each tank feeding its own engine, or a single tank feeding a single engine. The idea behind separate tanks for twin engines is sound. If one tank splits or becomes contaminated, the other tank and engine will not be affected, and by using cross-over valves both engines can run from either tank while the defective tank is isolated. In practice many boats have open balance pipes between the tanks, which negates this advantage.

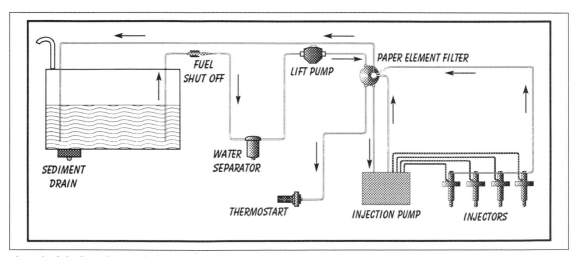

A typical fuel tank and fuel system arrangement.

The standard method of feeding fuel to each engine is to take the fuel inlet through the top of the tank. A drop-tube within the tank then extends down to a point an inch or so above the bottom. This leaves room for sediment to settle in the hope that it will not be drawn into the fuel line. There is occasionally a small sediment sump below the feed pipe with a drain cock or plug to make regular draining a possibility. I deliberately use the word 'possibility', as very few owners actually drain the sediment out of their fuel tanks, even when the facility is provided. In most cases the facility is not even provided.

The drawback with this conventional system is that no matter how well the tank is baffled to prevent excess fuel movement, once the fuel level drops below about 20 per cent of the tank's capacity it is impossible to prevent air entering the feed pipe during rough weather, due to the fuel slopping around violently within the tank. This means that a

fuel tank with a 200-gallon capacity must always carry 40 gallons of fuel that cannot reliably be used. This has been the standard arrangement on leisure craft for many years, yet it is both unreliable and a waste of space!

PERSHILLA'S TANK SYSTEM

Pershilla has a tank system that has proved to have many advantages over the more conventional systems although it is basically very simple. The fuel feed to both engines (and the diesel-fired hot-air heating system) is taken from the top of a small service tank with a capacity of 3 gallons. This is situated amidships on the engine compartment forward bulkhead below the level of the twin main tanks, which have a combined capacity of 300 gallons. These are situated on each side of the engine compartment. The fuel feeds are incorporated into a small inspection hatch on the

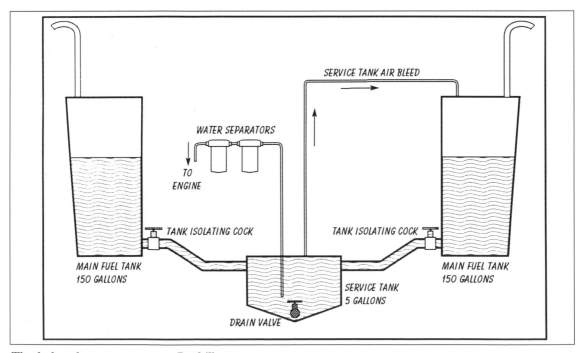

The fuel tank arrangement on Pershilla.

Fuel feeds on the service tank inspection hatch.

top of the service tank so that the interior of the tank can be inspected for corrosion at three-yearly intervals. Large inspection hatches are fitted to the front face of each main tank so that cleaning can also be performed easily every three years.

The bottom of the service tank is shaped into a 'V' form with a slope towards the front, where a 1in gate valve is fitted. Fuel is gravity-fed into the service tank via 1½in tubes from each of the main tanks and these tubes also act as balance pipes between the main tanks. Gate valves are fitted at the unions between the balance pipe and each main tank. When running, the main tank gate valves are closed to a quarter of their normal full open setting to slow the movement of fuel between the main tanks when rolling in rough weather and in fact are only fully opened during refuelling. Should one tank split or become contaminated it can

be isolated from the system in the normal way while fuel continues to feed the service tank from the other main tank. If required separate, service tanks can be installed for each engine although there is little point in this.

There is a fourth outlet on the top of the service tank, which is a permanent air bleed back to the main tanks designed to prevent the service tank becoming air-locked after draining or in the unlikely event of air finding its way in from either of the main tanks during rough weather.

With this system, it is possible to run the tanks down to the last 20 gallons with no fear of air entering the fuel feeds due to fuel slop within the main tanks. This represents a figure of 7.5 per cent of unusable fuel against the 20 per cent of the conventional system. Naturally I would never willingly let the fuel level get this low but in emergencies I would be able to keep the engines running longer than with a conventional system.

Draining the service tank is a simple matter of closing the gate valves on each of the main tanks, removing the stop plug in the end of the service tank drain valve and placing a large bucket beneath the outlet. The gate valve can then be fully opened and the contents of the tank drained into the bucket. The speed of escaping fuel through the 1in gate valve ensures that any sediment and water are flushed out into the bucket.

The gate valve is then closed and the stop plug replaced. The stop plug is fitted as a safeguard should the gate valve ever leak and is a standard precaution with large-capacity drain valves. The valves on the main tanks are opened last of all to refill the service tank and the clean fuel in the bucket is decanted back into the main tanks after the sediment and water has settled out.

I have installed this system onto two other boats: one a new build where the system was designed-in from new and another on a Freeman 33. On the Freeman the original standard system was modified with the fitting of service tanks below the level of the main tanks and the fuel feeds were then taken from the top of the service tanks.

MAKING UP A COMPRESSION JOINT

Any work on the fuel system will eventually require the making-up of compression joints. They are extremely reliable in terms of fuel-tight integrity, and being simple to assemble, they should always give perfect results. However, problems can and do occur when they are incorrectly assembled. The most common cause of problems is over-tightening.

There are several types of sealing ring (or olive) available, generally made of copper or brass. The most reliable in terms of effective joint sealing is the copper ring type as copper is very much softer than brass and therefore adapts more easily to the compressive pressure of tightening the securing nut.

Using a tube cutter for a clean cut.

To prepare a joint for assembly, the tube end must be cut off squarely, preferably using a proper tube cutter. These are cheap to buy at DIY stores and plumbers' merchants, and make pipework assembly very much quicker, especially where several joints are required. Using a tube cutter automatically ensures that the end of the tube is squarely cut and at the same time produces a small chamfer on the end of the tube. If a cutter is not available, a junior hacksaw used carefully will do the job but the end of the tube will need sanding to remove all burrs inside and out before assembly.

The end of the tube to be assembled must be straight, as it is vital that the tube enters the joint squarely. It is therefore good practice to have at least 2in (50mm) of straight tube before any bends. When bending tube by hand it is often difficult, if not impossible, to begin a bend close to the end of a tube without bending the end. A simple solution is to allow an extra 6in (150mm) or so of tube at the end

Different types of sealing ring (olive) and a dismantled fitting.

Assembling a joint.

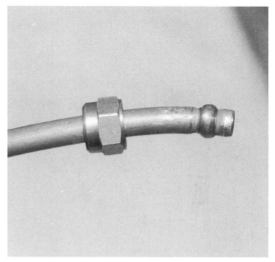

An over-tightened joint showing the distorted pipe.

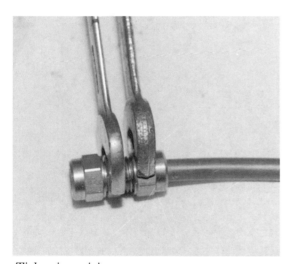

Tightening a joint.

where the fitting will be. After the bend is formed, cut off the excess length, leaving the required 2in of straight tubing between the fitting and the start of the bend.

To assemble the joint the nut is first slipped over the tube with the thread facing the fitting. This is followed by the copper ring. The tube end is then slipped into the fitting and pushed up against the flange inside. The copper ring is slid up against the face of the fitting, followed by the nut. Care must be taken to ensure the nut is correctly threaded onto the fitting before tightening by hand.

Tightening the nut with a spanner while holding the joint with another spanner completes the job. For small-bore fuel-line tube sizes, about one complete turn is sufficient to effect a perfect seal. Over-tightening only distorts the ring seal and crushes the pipe, inevitably causing the joint to leak. It is always better to under-tighten the joint as it can always be 'nipped up' later if there are any signs of leakage. When a perfect joint has been formed, it can be dismantled and reassembled many times and still form a perfect seal.

MODIFYING PERSHILLA

Modifying *Pershilla*'s fuel system to suit the Cummins was thankfully a straightforward procedure. The original $5/16$in copper tubing used by the Bedford had to be replaced with $1/2$in to suit the fuel flow of the Cummins. This

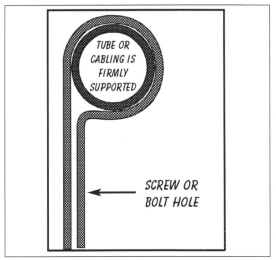

'P' clips can be used to support pipework or cabling.

Fuel filter elements. The large units to the left feed the Cummins, the smaller units feed the BMC wing engine.

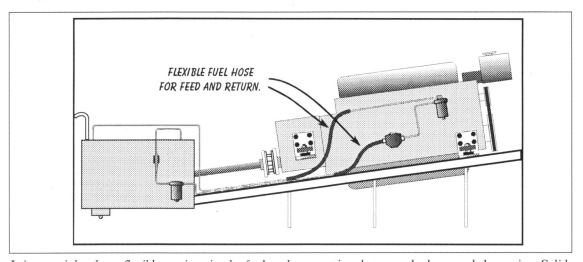

It is essential to have flexible sections in the feed and return pipes between the boat and the engine. Solid piping alone will eventually fracture due to the movement and vibrations of the engine.

was fastened to the side of the floor support using stainless steel 'P' clips. These have rubber inserts that hold the tube firmly without chafing. The CAV dual fuel-filter agglomeraters used for water separation and pre-filtering incorporated the standard-size CAV fuel filter elements. By fitting an adapter kit that allowed the filter heads to accept high capacity units, the fuel flow capacity was doubled, providing more than enough flow for the Cummins.

On smaller engine applications these double-size elements can be used to extend the interval between filter changes, especially where heavy contamination is present in the fuel. Cummins supplied flexible hoses for final

The Cummins fuel return 'tee'd' into the service tank bleed line (the rearmost tubing).

connection of the fixed copper piping to the engine as failure to use a flexible section eventually leads to fracture of the copper (or steel, or stainless steel), caused by vibration hardening.

The excess fuel return to the main tank required additional modification as the Cummins specification required the return pipe to drop to the bottom of the tank. This prevents frothing of the fuel on its return to the tank. The Bedford fuel return terminated inside the top of the tank and was therefore unsuitable. Although fuel frothing never gave us any problems, and returning the fuel via the top of the tank was until recently a fairly standard arrangement, I nevertheless modified the system in line with Cummins' specification.

Rather than removing one tank fitting and replacing it with a drop tube I re-routed the fuel return to the top of the service tank and joined it with a 'T' fitting into the air bleed from the service tank back to the main tank. Although this was a little unorthodox, it complied with the Cummins specification in every respect.

Other than these modifications the fuel system remained the same. Before removing

the inspection hatch from the service tank I drained the fuel and cleaned out the interior of the tank. There was a thin film of hard sediment in the 'V' bottom of the tank, and this was scraped out and wiped clean before the inspection hatch was refitted.

CHECKING THE PIPEWORK

In general terms, when the fuel system is modified or a new system is installed it is important to ensure that the fuel tubing is securely fixed so that it cannot vibrate. The first task is to plan the tubing runs so that they are safe from excess heat, such as generated by the area around the exhaust outlet, and also that they cannot be trodden on or otherwise damaged. There is more than one boat that has come to a stop because of the fuel feed being flattened by a careless size nine!

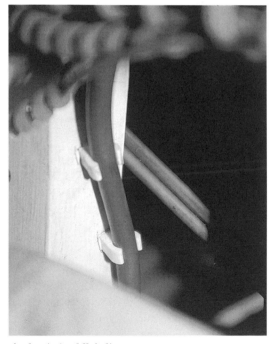

A plastic 'saddle' clip.

The issue of safeguarding the pipework is even more critical where petrol engines are being installed. With a diesel leak the worst problem is that of mess and smell. With a petrol leak there is the very grave danger of fire or explosion. Therefore any work on petrol engine fuel systems must be performed with extreme care.

Once the pipework route has been decided the tubing must be securely fastened to bulkheads to prevent vibration. There are various types of fastening for pipework, such as the 'P' clips used on *Pershilla*. Plastic snap-in fasteners of various types are also available, and although these do not have the same strength as 'P' clips, they do hold the pipework securely. They are available in a variety of sizes to suit differing tube sizes. Some types are also available in double and triple form for use where there are several pipe-runs side by side. The clip is screwed into position and the tubing is then pushed into the lugs, where it is held firmly.

Plastic two-way snap-in pipe clip.

THE EXHAUST SYSTEM

8

We looked at the problems of exhaust back pressure in Chapter 2. Where a turbo-charged engine is being installed it is essential for the exhaust system to be matched to the engine's power output. The manufacturer's recommendations for exhaust pipe cross-sectional area and length of pipe-run must be adhered to if full power and a smoke-free exhaust are to be achieved. The length of run may affect the required cross-sectional area of the exhaust tube, especially where very long runs are needed. The number of bends will also affect the tube area. It is therefore essential to keep the length of exhaust pipework to a minimum, with due regard to the design of vessel and engine installation.

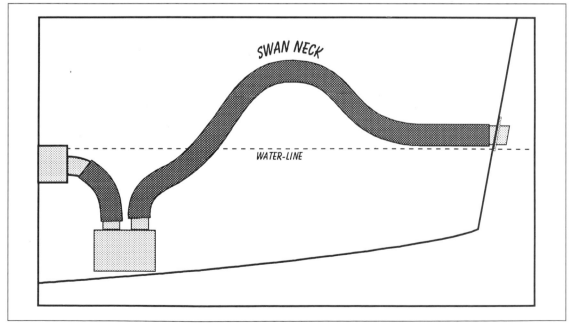

A swan-neck in the exhaust hose above the water-line prevents back flow from following waves entering the engine.

Another essential in the exhaust run is a swan-neck to prevent sea water forcing itself up through the exhaust and into the engine. This could occur if the engine was stopped and the boat was moored stern-to a following swell. The swan-neck is simply an inverted 'U' in the pipe-run that rises above the water-line to prevent this reverse flow of water.

Noise reduction is another area that needs careful consideration. Silencers can be another source of back pressure within the system, but if a monotonous drone is to be avoided they are essential. A properly designed silencer matched to the engine and length of exhaust piping will dramatically cut down noise without affecting the engine's performance. Yet another reason to consult the exhaust experts.

Water-cooled exhausts require a larger cross-sectional area than dry exhausts, as the water within the pipework reduces the usable volume available to the exhaust gases.

However, dry exhausts are generally restricted to older boats and working boats using a vertical exhaust stack through the roof. There are problems associated with dry exhausts, the most obvious being that of heat. With no breeze passing over the exhaust – as is the case in a car or truck – the pipework becomes extremely hot. It is therefore essential that all pipework is heavily lagged with heat insulation to prevent fire or injury. The same applies to certain parts of water-cooled exhausts, as there is always a short length of uncooled piping between the exhaust outlet and the water injection point.

On the majority of engines this length is very short but on some more specialized or unusual systems this uncooled section can be quite long. Engines that are mounted very low in the bilge with the exhaust outlet below the water-line must have a riser in the pipework to bring the water injection point above the water-line. This ensures that the injected

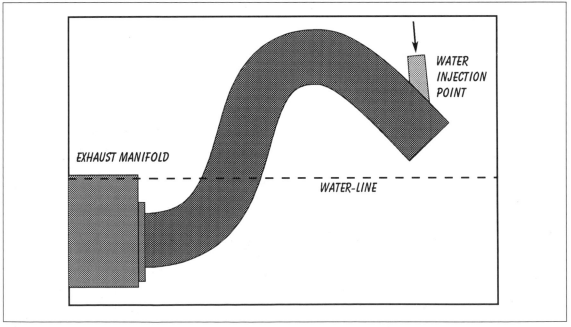

Engines installed below the water-line may need an exhaust 'riser' between the manifold and the water injection point.

cooling water cannot run back into the engine. It also prevents flooding of the engine caused by siphoning via the water pump. Whatever the reason for the riser it must be lagged in the same way as a dry exhaust and wiring and fuel piping within the vicinity must be re-routed away from this source of heat. This is particularly important with the fuel piping of petrol installations.

PERSHILLA'S EXHAUST SYSTEM

Pershilla's exhaust system was carefully designed with the assistance of Halyard Marine during the planning process, and apart from the usual struggle with the tenacious exhaust hose it did not reveal any unpleasant surprises. I had prepared the watertight fitting to take the exhaust through the bulkhead from the engine compartment to the aft cabin while the engine compartment was empty. Once the engine was in position I was able to set up the exhaust pipe-runs within the engine compartment. Prior to this I could not fit the through-bulkhead watertight fitting, as I was not sure of the angle it would need to adopt to provide a smooth exhaust hose run.

The Halyard water-lock silencer was substantially larger than the plastic Vetus silencer it replaced. Nevertheless there was still just sufficient room for it next to the bulkhead. I fabricated a ply base for it to sit on and secured it to the bulkhead with stainless steel strapping.

The 5in hose from the engine to the silencer was next cut to length and fitted, first

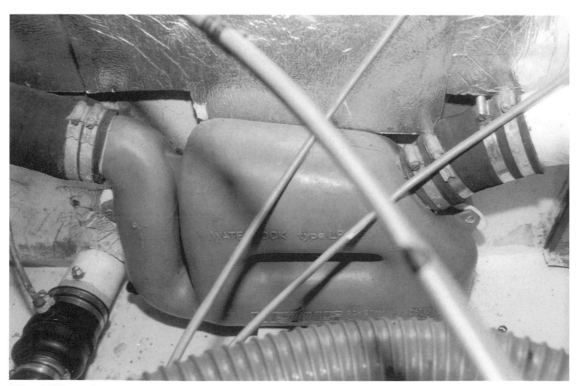

The old Vetus silencer used with the Bedford.

The new Halyard Marine silencer with pipework connected.

The four-drawer chest in the aft cabin with the 6in hose running alongside.

to the exhaust injection elbow on the engine and then round and onto the inlet in the side of the silencer. With the through-bulkhead elbow set roughly in position I measured the distance between it and the 6in outlet on top of the silencer along the line of the proposed pipe-run. Care was needed here before cutting the tube as there was very little margin for error and 6in exhaust tube does not come cheaply!

After double-checking the measurement and allowing 3in (75mm) for mistakes I gingerly cut the tube and offered it up. With the extra 3in the length was just about right. I fitted one end onto the silencer and fastened it with a clamp to prevent it pulling off while bending the hose through 90 degrees to connect with the bulkhead fitting. I then moved into the aft cabin and measured the distance between the bulkhead fitting and the transom outlet, which had been installed during the general preparation work. As this was a long run I decided against cutting the hose until I could offer it up in position rather than trying to get an accurate measurement with the tape rule.

The drawer in the cabinet had already been removed and the timber facia cut away to

allow the 6in hose to pass through to the bulkhead. At this stage I was not trying to compress it into the ellipse we discussed in Chapter 2. I therefore had to make the cut-out large enough to take the full 6in diameter. The hose was eventually slid past the cabinet and up towards the bulkhead. As soon as it was past the back of the cabinet it had to make a 90-degree bend to connect with the bulkhead fitting. Access to this area was made easy by having a removable back to the storage locker next to the cabinet. I was therefore able to

The custom-made stainless steel dual-exhaust outlet.

crawl inside, and with a friend feeding the hose through I was able to pull it into position and slip it onto the through-bulkhead fitting.

The other end of the exhaust hose was lying in a large loop on the bed. By forming it into a swan-neck we were able to force the free end into the enlarged hole in the face of the bedside cabinet and then into the space under the bed. It now had to sweep upwards to the inboard end of the stainless steel transom fitting. It was about 6in (150mm) too long to lie in a neat run so we pulled the end into the bed space and cut off 4in (100mm) before trying it for length again. This time we were able to slip the end onto the flange until the hose lay flat on the floor under the bed. The original 2in exhaust hose of the wing engine was then refitted alongside the new 6in hose. Heavy-duty bolted hose clamps were used in pairs for securing the 6in hose, as ordinary

hose clips are not robust enough for larger sizes. The wing engine exhaust, however, was reconnected using standard 2in hose clips.

The drawer unit could now be reassembled, but the first job was to flatten the hose into a 3in-wide ellipse to allow the drawers to be refitted. The internal stiffening wire inside the hose was flattened by hammering on a piece of ply to protect the skin of the hose from damage. Once the shape was formed the new side of the cabinet was fitted and screwed into position, where it held the hose in shape. After repainting the inside, the drawer runners were refitted and the face of the cabinet remade to suit the size of the new drawer. As the face of the cabinet was covered with carpet that had previously been peeled back prior to enlarging the hose access, all that was required now was to glue it back into place. The final join was virtually undetectable.

Internal view of the transom exhaust fitting.

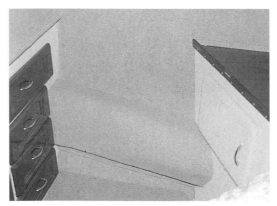

The exhaust trimmed with carpet and the four-drawer chest reassembled.

THE ELECTRICAL SYSTEM

9

In a repowering project the electrical system should not require too much modification. The areas that do need careful attention to detail are the starting and charging circuits. Where a much larger engine is being installed it is fair to assume that greater starting current will be required to spin it over on the starter motor. The capacity of the battery is the first item to check to ensure that it is man enough for the job. The engine manufacturer will supply the required specification for the starting battery.

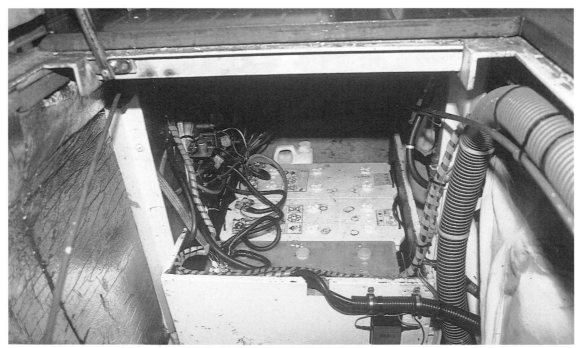

A heavy-duty battery box with the lid removed for clarity. It is built from $^3/_4$in exterior ply and fibre-glassed internally.

THE RIGHT STARTING BATTERY

There are several different classification systems applying to batteries, all providing the same information in different forms. I always refer to the CCA (cold cranking amps) standard when looking at batteries. This refers to the maximum amperage of the battery for starting a cold engine – 1,000 amps is about the maximum found on standard truck batteries, and this is sufficient for starting the average boat diesel.

Some older diesel engines required greater cranking power than their modern counterparts because of the outmoded design of their starter motors. It may well be that a modern large-capacity engine will require the same battery capacity or less than the old engine it

is replacing. However, check with the manufacturer. Good-quality, heavy-duty commercial vehicle batteries are ideal for boat use and are very economically priced compared to specialist marine batteries. However, many people prefer the maintenance-free types that are also spill-proof. There are several types of battery available for special purposes but for all-round economy and a long and reliable life, good-quality lorry batteries are hard to beat.

There are several necessary steps to take to ensure long battery life. The first concerns the battery box in which they are secured. This must be strong enough to hold the batteries securely in place in all weathers and should ideally have a fitted lid to prevent metal objects dropping on to the terminals. The lid must be ventilated to allow gases from the charging process to escape, thus preventing dangerous accumulations from building up. A

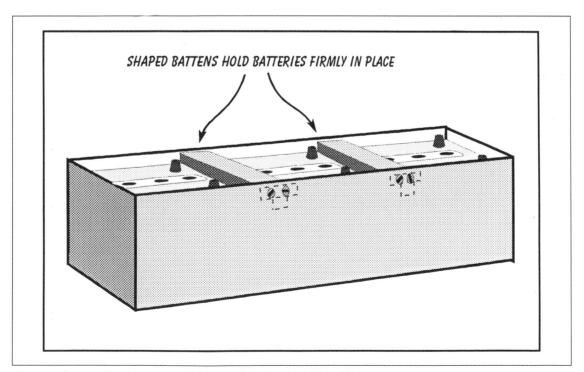

A strong battery box is an essential part of the electrical installation.

box constructed of ³/₄in ply with a fibre-glass mat/resin lining is ideal for the purpose. The battery terminals need cleaning and greasing at least once a season and the electrolyte level should be checked and topped up if necessary at least once a month.

STARTER CABLES

Once the starting battery size has been decided, the next item to check is the starter cables. These need to be of sufficient cross-sectional area to carry the maximum current required by the starter motor without a significant voltage drop. Long cable runs require a greater cross-sectional area but in any case it is always advisable to keep the cable runs as short as possible. Obviously the positive and negative leads must be of the same cross-sectional area to prevent voltage drop and overheating of the cables.

Good earthing is vital to the overall performance of the electrical system. Terminals for the starter cables should be of heavy-duty construction and preferably bolted and soldered. Crimp terminals are not sufficient for heavy current loads.

ISOLATING SWITCHES

A high-quality battery isolating switch should be installed in each battery positive main feed, unless any batteries are constantly operated in parallel, in which case one switch will suffice for the two. It is bad practice to fit an isolating switch in the negative earth line to cover all the batteries rather than one for each battery in the positive feed. For one thing this can affect overall performance of the electrical system by reducing the effectiveness of the earth connection.

There are many battery switches on the market, most of which are incapable of carrying the starting current of a large engine. Cheap isolating switches are a false economy as they can affect the performance of the electrical system and may damage the alternator if the internal connections should fail, as they have been known to do. Isolating switches for starter cables are obtainable from specialist marine electrical stockists such as Adverc BM, who can supply the correct switch to handle the current load. Chandlers generally do not have the in-depth knowledge to advise on electrical installations. Marine electronics specialists, on the other hand, will be happy to

A heavy-duty battery isolating switch capable of carrying starting current.

A good quality 'one-two-off' battery selector and isolating switch.

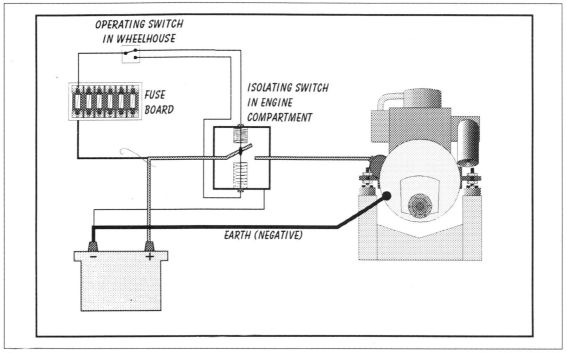

Diagrammatic view of a remotely operated battery isolating switch.

advise on the correct installation procedure and the right equipment to use.

It is not a good idea to route starting circuits up into the accommodation just to position the isolating switch in a convenient position. This considerably increases the cable length and therefore reduces starter performance. The ideal place for the starting circuit isolating switch is close to the battery. This means there is no additional cable length and also provides a certain level of security, as it becomes impossible to start the engines until this switch is placed in the on position.

Where it is imperative to have the starting circuit isolating switch in the wheelhouse, remote controlled switches are available. These do not require additional cable runs as the isolating switch itself is located down by the batteries. A remotely mounted operating switch can then be fitted in a convenient position in the wheelhouse. This type of switch is in effect a large relay as the main switch that carries the heavy current is opened or closed by a low-current switching mechanism. They are very expensive when compared with manually operated switches and carry the additional danger that the operating switch may be inadvertently switched off when the engine is running, thereby damaging the alternator. To prevent this happening it is good practice to fit a cover over the operating switch.

THE ALTERNATOR REGULATOR

The new engine may be fitted with a more powerful alternator than the original. This means checking the wiring of the charging circuit to ensure it is of adequate size for the

Adverc alternator regulator module.

Older versions of the Adverc required the standard regulator to be removed and a brush holder fitted in its place.

The latest Advercs use a modified standard regulator.

maximum output of the alternator. To ensure that the battery charging system is working to its full capacity it may be a good time to consider installing an external alternator regulator. The best known of these is the Adverc, which can be installed in a few hours.

These provide several major improvements over the standard alternator regulator, the most important of which is the ability to charge the battery up to 100 per cent capacity. An alternator with a standard regulator can never fully charge the batteries due to the 'counter voltage' that builds up in the batteries during the discharge and recharging processes. The regulator fitted as standard to all vehicle alternators is set to a nominal 14.0–14.2 volts (± 0.4 volts). This is insufficient to overcome the counter voltage that builds up in the battery and restricts recharging to about 70 per cent of the battery's capacity.

The Adverc regulator allows the battery voltages to rise temporarily to 14.4 volts, thus overcoming counter voltage and bringing the battery up to a 100 per cent state of charge without allowing the batteries to gas.

Another major advantage of the external regulator is that it converts the alternator from machine-sensing to battery-sensing. Machine-sensed alternators check the state of charge at the alternator itself. Unfortunately this does not allow for losses in the wiring system, so the alternator is never aware of the real state of charge. Battery-sensed alternators check the state of charge at the battery itself and so any losses within the wiring are ignored. The alternator can then provide the output necessary to bring the battery up to full charge by overcoming losses in the system.

This is particularly important where blocking diodes are used in a split-charging system, as there is a voltage drop through most

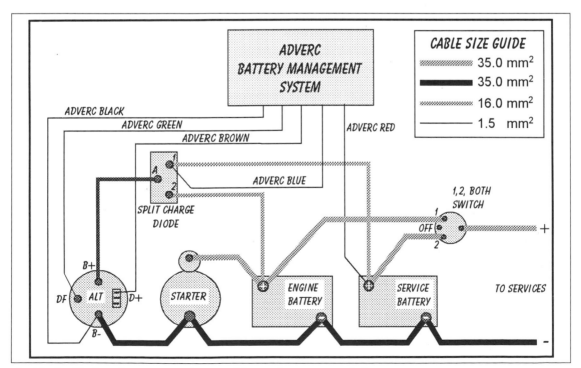

An ideal split charging system using an Adverc alternator regulating system.

diodes of about 0.9 volts. With a standard regulator this is sufficient to prevent proper charging even to 70 per cent capacity. The external regulator controls the output of the alternator to provide the battery with the rate of charge required regardless of any intervening losses. An external alternator regulator combined with a split-charge system will ensure that the electrical system is always in good condition and ready to start the engine.

STOP SOLENOIDS

Ensuring the engine will start is of first importance, but of equal importance is the need to stop it. Most modern engines are provided with electric solenoids to stop the engine. These are easier to operate than a pull-cable and make it simpler to arrange engine stops at all control positions. All that is required on the fly-bridge, for example, is another stop button.

Despite the advantages of the stop solenoid a word of caution is required regarding which type to use. There are two types of stop solenoid: energize to start and energize to stop. The first is the type used on diesel cars, where the solenoid is switched on when the key is turned to start the engine. It then remains in the 'run' position until the key is turned off and the engine stops. This gives the diesel car driver the same convenience as the petrol car driver.

However, this system is totally unsuitable for boat use and it does not take much imagination to work out why. One of the biggest benefits of the marine diesel engine is that it does not require an electrical supply to enable it to run. This theoretically makes it 50 per cent more reliable than the petrol engine. If an energize to start solenoid is introduced to the engine it then *does* require an electrical supply to enable it to run, resulting in an immediate 50 per cent loss of reliability! If the

boat were to be partially swamped and the electrical system were to fail, the engine would immediately stop, and with no battery power would never start again.

Clearly the only option for marine diesel engines is the energize to stop solenoid. This is simply coupled to the stop lever on the injection pump in place of the manual pull-cable. When any stop button is pressed the solenoid pulls the lever to the stop position and the engine stops. Once the stop button is released, the solenoid allows the lever to return to the run position ready for the next start. In this situation, if the boat is swamped but the engine is still receiving clean fuel and is above water, it will continue to run.

STARTING AIDS

To return to the subject of starting, let us look at cold weather starting. There are two main types of cold starting aid in use today on small boat engines. These are the combustion chamber heaters generally found on indirect-injection engines and the fuel-fed Thermostart found on larger-capacity, direct-injection engines. The word 'Thermostart' should not be confused with 'thermostat', a completely different piece of equipment.

Combustion Chamber Heaters

Combustion chamber heaters are screw fitted into each combustion chamber of the engine and are in fact miniature electric fires with a heating element that glows red hot when the heaters are switched on. The drawback with these is that they have a limited life if they are inadvertently operated while turning the engine over on the starter. The element becomes fragile while hot and the pressures within the combustion chamber can break it. The other drawback is that if they are left screwed into place for many years they have a tendency to break off when being unscrewed for replacement. When this happens the cylinder head must be removed to allow the broken section to be taken out. It is at this point that many owners will resort to using a starting fluid such as Easy Start rather than make the effort to remove the head.

For emergencies or very occasional use these starting fluids are acceptable but they should not be used continually because of the drying effect the fluid has on the cylinder walls – this increases bore wear. The other problem is that if too much fluid is sprayed into the inlet, the resulting explosion stops the piston dead on its upward stroke and causes excessive strain on the crankshaft and bearings. Lubricants are included in the ingredients of starting fluids to help avoid the dry cylinder problem, but nothing can be done to stop over-zealous spraying. It may be possible to provide a can with a metered amount of fluid per spray, but even then many people would simply spray it three or four times with the same result. The safest procedure is to keep the starting fluid strictly for emergencies and then use it as sparingly as possible. For general starting it is far better to ensure that the preheating system operates correctly.

Where combustion chamber heaters are fitted it is good practice to remove them annually to clean the threads of corrosion and the heating elements of any carbon deposits. If the threads are then coated with an anti-seize compound such as Copperease they will be easy to remove when the time comes for replacement.

The Thermostart

While combustion chamber heaters are simple devices, the Thermostart is rather more complex as it not only requires an electrical feed but also a fuel feed. Thermostarts fitted to early engines used a reservoir with a tap for

A Thermostart cold starting aid.

the fuel feed. The reservoir needed topping up occasionally by the owner and the tap was designed to be turned off after every use. On later models a reservoir was developed that filled automatically from the engine's fuel system. This included an overflow back to the fuel tank so that the owner no longer had to top it up manually. It was also found that the tap was no longer required. More recently it has been discovered that the reservoir is not required at all and on modern engines the Thermostart is simply connected into one of the spare outlets on the engine fuel filter so that the pressure of the lift pump feeds the fuel when the valve is open.

No matter how the fuel is fed to the Thermostart, they all operate in exactly the same way. The Thermostart itself consists of a heating element attached to a ball valve. As the element becomes heated, it expands and opens the valve to allow fuel to flow onto the element. As soon as the engine turns over on the starter the air flowing over the fuel-soaked element causes it to burst into flames. These are drawn into the cylinder to provide an immediate heat source to aid initial combustion. The concept sounds somewhat

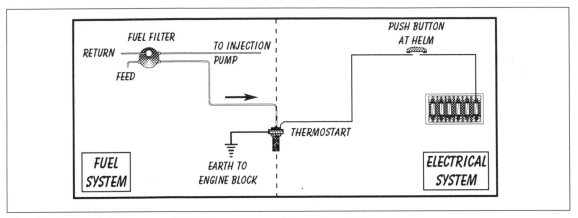

The electrical and fuel system of the Thermostart cold starting aid.

crude, but these devices are exceptionally effective and generally have a very reliable and long life.

PERSHILLA

The locations of all the main electrical components on the Cummins were virtually identical to those on the Bedford. Reconnecting the various items was mainly a matter of extending existing cables. The water temperature gauge and high temperature warning senders needed their cables extending to reach the loom, but by using crimp terminals the job was quick, neat and reliable. The starter cable used for the Bedford was larger than the specified size for the Cummins so this was retained and connected directly to the Cummins starter motor. As I was using the original alternator from the Bedford with the Adverc external regulator, the cables were already correctly terminated and ready to be reconnected.

The only electrical items to be changed were the oil pressure and water temperature gauges in the wheelhouse and on the flybridge. The main reason for this change was

that the Yazaki instruments already installed were no longer available and I did not want to use second-hand senders in the new engine. I therefore specified Cummins standard VDO gauges as replacements. Normally each engine is supplied with a complete instrument panel, but as I did not intend to modify the original custom-built panel, I merely opted for new oil pressure and water temperature gauges and retained the rest of the original instruments.

New VDO gauges installed on the far left of Pershilla's instrument panel.

THE COOLING SYSTEM 10

All large marine engines in normal use are water-cooled, using either a standard heat exchanger arrangement or the less common keel cooling for specialized applications. Both methods use a mixture of fresh water and anti-freeze to circulate through the engine block with the advantage that corrosion inhibitors can be added to the water for year-round engine protection.

Raw-water cooling takes the water straight out of the river or sea to circulate through the block and is still in use on old engines and some modern petrol engines. The corrosion and cold running problems that this system creates make it unacceptable for serious cruising vessels.

DIRECT OR RAW-WATER COOLING

The only advantage of raw-water cooling is the reduced cost of the marinizing parts required. The system takes raw water directly out of the sea or river, circulates it round the engine block and finally discharges it overboard, usually via the exhaust pipework. There are many drawbacks to this system, making it totally unsuitable for use with a modern, high-powered diesel engine. A standard thermostat that allows the engine to run at its correct temperature of around 80°C cannot be used as this causes blockages to occur in the water passages from the build-up of impurities and silt on the walls.

The usual recommended working temperature for a direct-cooled engine is about 54°C. This low temperature causes sludging of the lubricating oil, as it never reaches optimum working temperature, resulting in increased engine wear. The low temperature also means that ancillary items like the calorifier for domestic water heating cannot be used effectively. However, the most important problem is the corrosion products produced by the hot raw water that continually attack the engine's

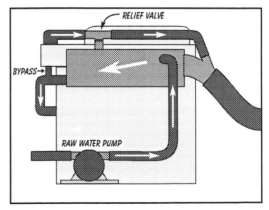

A simple raw-water cooling system. The only advantage is its cheapness.

internal passageways. Obviously it is impossible to combat this with corrosion inhibitors. The entire cooling system must also be carefully drained during the winter months to prevent frost damage as anti-freeze cannot be added.

Raw-water cooling equipment consists of an impeller-type water pump and water-cooled manifold plus a marine gearbox, either mechanical or hydraulic, and a gearbox oil-cooler if required.

INDIRECT OR FRESHWATER COOLING

None of the problems mentioned above occur with indirectly cooled engines. These have a separate freshwater supply within the engine block in the manner for which the engine was designed. This allows anti-freeze and corrosion inhibitors to be added to the freshwater

supply, thus preventing the problems that beset crude, raw-water-cooled engines. A standard 80°C thermostat is used to ensure the engine runs at the intended temperature. This provides maximum running efficiency, long life and also allows the use of a calorifier to supply free domestic hot water. Additional equipment required for indirect cooling includes a heat exchanger (often combined with the water-cooled manifold) and an engine oil-cooler if required.

The Heat Exchanger

This piece of equipment performs the same function as the radiator in a vehicle by cooling the water flowing round the engine block. In a radiator it is air that is forced through the matrix by either the forward motion of the car or the engine fan that removes the excess heat. With a heat exchanger it is raw water (drawn in from the sea or river by the raw-water

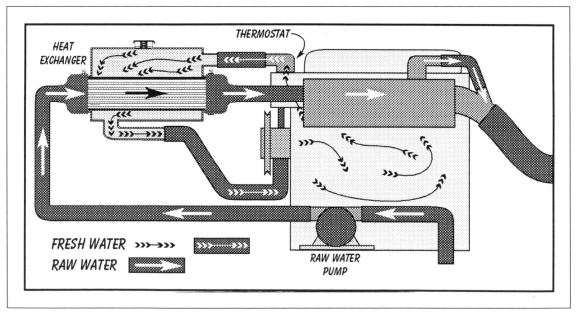

The more complex freshwater cooling system protects the engine from corrosion and allows correct temperature running for low wear and efficiency.

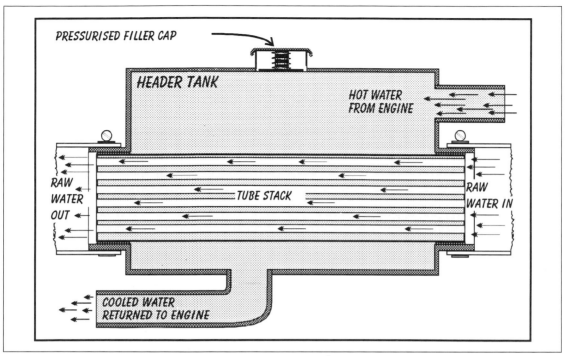

Cross-section through a heat exchanger.

pump) that removes the excess heat. It does this by circulating the fresh water (the water in the block) around a tightly packed tube stack in the heat exchanger body. The raw water passes through the tubes and absorbs the heat before entering the exhaust pipe and being discharged overboard back into the sea.

The tube stack is similar to that found in a steam engine boiler although the tubes in the heat exchanger are more tightly packed to give maximum cooling effect. The ends of the tube stack are sealed to prevent raw water mixing with the fresh. This makes it possible to add anti-freeze and anti-corrosives to the system to keep the engine block in tip-top condition. It is important to have a reliable raw-water inlet strainer as the tubes can quickly become clogged if mud and weed are allowed to reach them. Part of the annual service should be to clean out the tubes by gently rodding through

with a suitable piece of stiff wire such as the trusty wire coat-hanger!

For repair or replacement the complete stack is removable. The ends of the stack are revealed by removing the end covers from the heat exchanger. This is either a neoprene type secured with hose clips or a metal plate with an 'O' ring seal secured with bolts. Combined heat exchanger manifolds used on smaller engines directly replace the old exhaust manifold while the larger, single-unit heat exchanger usually bolts on to the front of the engine and may require additional support brackets.

Water-Cooled Exhaust Manifolds

Vehicle exhausts are cooled by air but as anyone who has accidentally touched one after a drive will know they still become extremely

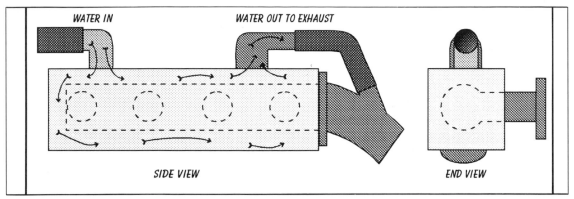

Cross-section through a water-cooled manifold.

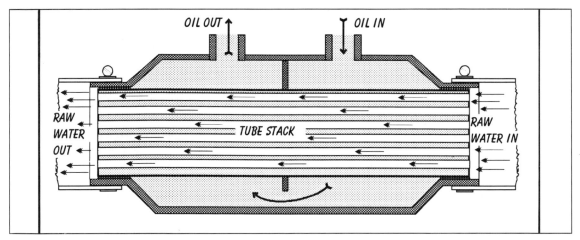

Cross-section through an oil-cooler.

hot! Without the cooling influence of the air they would be quite capable of starting a fire, hence the need for water cooling in marine installations. The water-cooled manifold itself is a fairly simple construction, consisting of a water jacket surrounding the manifold. This keeps the temperature down to acceptable levels where there is no fire risk.

Oil-Cooler

This is often a smaller version of the heat exchanger with a tube stack through which the cooling water passes. Some modern engines such as the Cummins have the oil-cooler built into the block. Engine oil taken via a special adapter (usually at the oil-filter block) is pumped around the tubes and cooled. There are fewer tubes in the oil-cooler as the oil does not require the same degree of cooling as the circulating water in the heat exchanger; indeed if the oil is over-cooled the problem of sludging and reduced lubricating efficiency can occur.

RAW-WATER PUMP

These are almost universally of the flexible impeller type, which are very reliable and

A raw-water pump impeller. Note how the splines are bent away from the direction of running.

powerful for their size. As the name implies they are fitted on the raw-water system and are in addition to the standard engine circulating pump on the freshwater system. They are used to draw in cooling water from the river or sea for heat exchanger, exhaust manifold and oil-cooling purposes. Jabsco, the name of the inventor of this type of pump, has become the generic term for flexible impeller pumps in the same way that Hoover has for vacuum cleaners. However, Johnson and Sherwood pumps are equally reliable.

Neoprene impellers are standard for normal use and they rely on the water passing through the pump for cooling and lubrication. Great care must be exercised to ensure they never run dry, as this leads to rapid impeller failure (in a matter of minutes). Even with a new engine it is essential to keep a spare impeller on board and know how to change it. It is a recognized part of the laying-up procedure at the end of the season to remove the impeller to prevent it freezing into place or permanently distorting.

KEEL- AND TANK-COOLING

Keel-cooling is generally only necessary in special circumstances, for example where the water is badly polluted. There are two methods

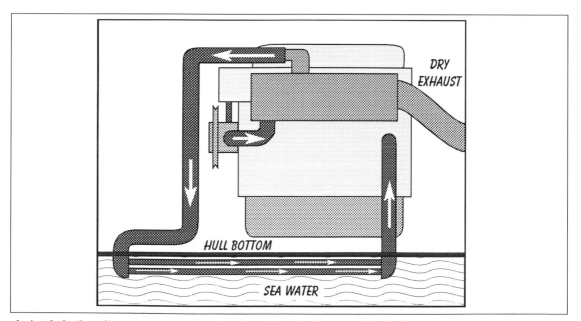

A simple keel-cooling arrangement using tubes along the bottom of the hull.

used. The most efficient but most vulnerable to damage is to run heavy-duty cooling pipes along the outside of the bottom of the hull. The engine-circulating water passes through the tubes and is cooled by the river or sea water outside the tubes. The main problem with this system is the vulnerability of the outside pipework to damage from hitting underwater obstructions.

The other method is to build a skin tank into the bottom of the boat and circulate the engine water through this. The cooling effect is achieved by the sea or river water passing under the boat outside the skin tank. Because the cooling area of the bottom of the skin tank is restricted, this system is less efficient. It can also only be used on steel-construction vessels.

With either method a dry exhaust system is necessary unless provision is made to draw in water solely for exhaust cooling, but this would negate the main advantage of the system.

CORROSION PROTECTION

We have already discussed the coolant additives that care for the inside of the engine

block, but there is also a need to look after the raw-water side of the system. Modern engines have built-in corrosion protection in the form of small zinc anodes screwed into various parts of the raw-water system. On the Cummins there is one in the end of the heat exchanger and two in the raw-water-cooled after-cooler. All they require is an annual check on their condition to see how far they have corroded. Once they are about half gone they should be replaced in the same manner as hull-protection anodes. If they appear to corrode fairly rapidly, do not be tempted to avoid replacement. They are doing their job of protecting the engine cooling system, which would otherwise be corroding instead!

VENTILATION

It should be remembered that the flow of air into the engine compartment is a vital part of the cooling system as well as being vital to the combustion process. Engine manufacturers specify the minimum cross-sectional area of engine compartment vents, and for a powerful engine this is a large area. The ambient temperature of the engine compartment affects the

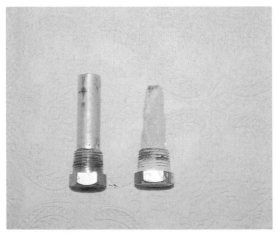

Zinc pencil anodes; new on the left, old on the right.

Ventilation fans installed in the engine compartment to overcome problems of small air-intakes.

running temperature of the engine as well as the performance, making it vital to provide the required amount of air. If the specified cross-sectional area of the air vents cannot be achieved, it is permissible to increase the air input by forced ventilation using fans. The engine manufacturers will specify the required air flow for fan-assisted ventilation.

PERSHILLA

In contrast to the exhaust, adapting the raw-water system was simple and relatively inexpensive. The Bedford needed a standard $1^{1}/_{4}$in skin fitting for the water inlet while the Cummins demanded a 2in fitting with integral scoop. While changing the fitting I also took the opportunity to substitute the gate valves on both the main and wing engine water inlets for quick-action ball valves, which are easy to operate and require no maintenance.

The original $1^{1}/_{2}$in Vetus water strainer was replaced with a larger-capacity 2in version from the same company while the pipework was uprated to 2in and re-routed to suit the location of the raw-water pump on the

Cummins. The water strainers are mounted on the aft-cabin side of the aft bulkhead just below floor level beneath a hatch in the wheelhouse floor.

They are positioned here for two reasons. Firstly the inlet pipework is out of the engine compartment and therefore protected from fire risk, and secondly the water strainers are very easy to get at for cleaning without leaving the wheelhouse.

The final job on the water-cooling system was to run a water feed from the tapped outlet under the exhaust water injection elbow to the Deep Sea Seal on the propeller shaft.

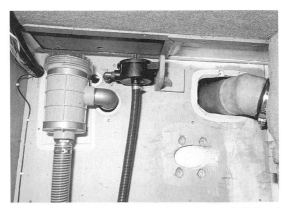

Raw-water strainers mounted on the aft bulkhead outside the engine compartment. Note the through-bulkhead exhaust elbow to the right of the picture.

The raw-water strainers are easily accessible for cleaning through a hatch in the wheelhouse floor.

Pershilla's Ventilation

Moving on to the ventilation system, *Pershilla*'s air inlet vents were woefully inadequate for the Cummins. With hindsight they were probably inadequate for the Bedford, but without cutting great slabs out of the sides of the hull there was no practical way to enlarge them. I therefore opted for the forced air system. Unfortunately this has one main drawback, which is that when the engine is running on low revs there is more air entering the compartment than is being used by the engine so the compartment becomes slightly pressurised. This forces fumes from the engine compartment into the wheelhouse, and although this is not dangerous, it is a little unpleasant. The only way to overcome this is to switch off the fans when running at low revs as there is much less demand for air within the compartment. I would eventually like to arrange an automatic method of switching off the fans at a preset rev limit, but this is currently low on the list of priorities.

11

SOUND-PROOFING THE ENGINE ROOM

If the vessel being repowered is more than about fifteen years old, it is quite likely that the level of engine compartment sound-proofing leaves a lot to be desired. For many years this was an issue that many boat builders chose to ignore, apparently considering it to be of little importance. Many owners at the time were probably less discerning and were prepared to accept high noise levels as a normal part of motor boating.

Not only does excess noise spoil the pleasure of boating, it also leads to stress and loss of concentration, especially on long passages. High noise levels prevent the proper monitoring of radio transmissions and make conversation between crew members difficult and unpleasant. Builders of luxury (priced) craft usually made more effort to reduce noise levels, but it is only in very recent years that the subject has begun to be treated with the

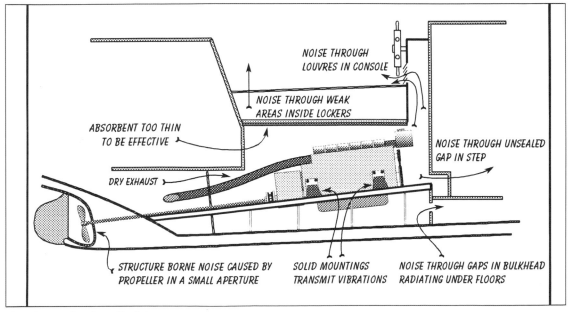

A noisy engine installation.

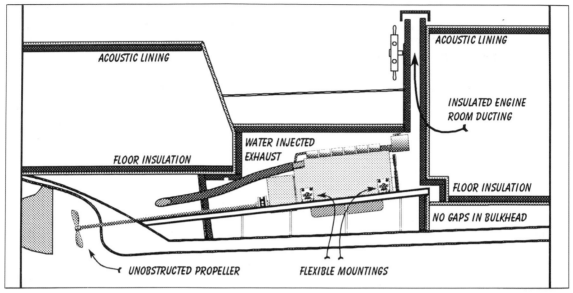

A quiet engine installation.

importance it deserves. Even now the work is often restricted to the simple process of fitting sound-absorbing materials and some soft rubber around the hatch edges. These two measures do not greatly reduce sound levels unless they are used as part of a planned strategy.

All in all, if the boat was noisy before beginning the repowering project, now is a good time to deal with the problem as part of the package.

Even the most expensive sound-absorbing materials will prove to be disappointingly ineffective if used without first studying the problem of noise transmission as a whole. It does not require a degree in physics to understand what is happening and I do not intend to quote meaningless columns of figures to illustrate a simple point in complex terms.

TYPES OF SOUND EMISSION

For a sound-proofing scheme to be effective it is essential for the installer – in this case the owner – to have an insight into how sound travels. A little basic common sense, which practically minded boat owners seem to be blessed with, is all that is required.

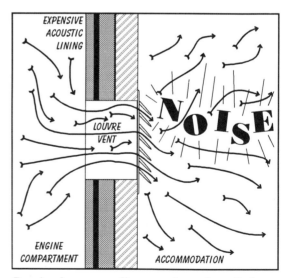

Despite the surrounding sound-proofing all the noise rushes out of the unguarded opening in the louvre vent.

Basically there are two types of sound emission to contend with, the most obvious being the airborne mechanical noise produced by the running engine. If not contained and absorbed it is carried through the boat. This is the starting point for planning the strategy of containment and absorption.

A simple analogy is to compare sound with water. Bear in mind that even a small opening in the engine compartment will allow sound to escape in volumes out of all proportion to the size of the opening. This makes it essential to close off every opening, however small, and to seal down all hatches with soft rubber or sponge sealing strip. This is the containment phase.

The other type of noise emanates from reverberating panels, especially those on steel boats. This reverberation is generally caused by airborne noise within the engine compartment striking the inner face of a panel. This sets up vibrations that produce further sounds to be carried along with the rest of the cacophony.

Sound containment is most effectively achieved in a small area. If the engine is sitting in the centre of a huge empty bilge space, the first job, if at all feasible, is to box it in as closely as possible while still maintaining easy access for servicing and maintenance. Diesel generators supplied in sound-proofed cocoons for installation in engine compartments are a good example of what can be achieved, as they tend to be almost inaudible when properly installed.

However, in most cases where big engines are involved it is impractical to box the engine in closely in this manner so the next best thing

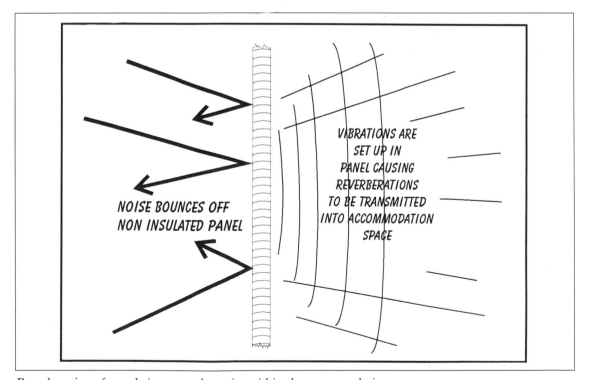

Reverberation of panels increases the noise within the accommodation.

is to insulate the entire engine compartment to a high standard. The minimum acceptable thickness of ply for engine compartment bulkheads and panels is $1/2$in, with $3/4$in being preferable.

Sound-absorbing materials must be fitted to *all* the inner faces of the compartment, including the hull sides if these form the sides of the compartment. Remember, the purpose of these materials is to *absorb* noise, and any hard surfaces left uncovered will simply reflect and amplify the noise. The proprietary brands of sound-proofing that utilize lead sheeting as part of a laminate of differing grades of foam are by far the most effective. The density of the lead prevents the panel from reverberating and causing further noises, while the foam layers act as an absorption medium for the airborne engine noise.

This is the absorption phase. It is also possible to glue heavy rubber matting into the bilges to prevent vibrations and echoes from these panels but this is probably too extreme a measure for the average boat owner.

HOME-MADE SOUND-PROOFING

Although proprietary brands of sound-proofing are very effective they are also very expensive. However, with a little care it is quite feasible to sound-proof an engine compartment to an equally high standard for about 20 per cent of the cost of buying the real thing. Proprietary brands of sound-proofing will provide a superior result but only if the techniques described here are applied to the rest of the job.

The cheapest form of DIY sound-proofing is made up using domestic fibre-glass loft insulation or Rockwool, peg-board and bitumastic paint. Peg-board, for anyone unfamiliar with the name, is simply hardboard sheet drilled every two inches with small holes.

The holes are necessary to allow sound to enter the insulation and be absorbed. Another option, although slightly more expensive than peg-board, is expanded aluminium mesh. The bitumastic paint takes the place of the lead layer in the foam insulation and acts to deaden the panel in the same way.

Whichever material is chosen – expensive foam sheeting or cheap fibre-glass Rockwool – it cannot be over-emphasized that it is vital for all openings in the engine compartment to be sealed. Even the most expensive of sound-proofing materials is useless if sound simply bypasses it and escapes. All removable panels must therefore be laid down (and preferably secured) on soft rubber or neoprene strip to contain the noise.

I often see cases where the most expensive lead-lined sound insulation has been applied in an engine compartment but the engine ventilation has been provided by louvre vents fitted into the compartment side panels. The result is that the only thing to be reduced significantly is the owner's bank balance!

The basis of an effective sound insulation scheme is preventing engine noise within the compartment reverberating around inside, and echoing off hard surfaces to amplify the noise. The absorption qualities of the insulation material must therefore deal effectively with this aspect. The next stage is to prevent the panels and bulkheads of the compartment itself from vibrating and transmitting further noises through the air. Again, the insulation material should deal with this through the inert lead or bitumastic layer within the laminate, which prevents vibrations from starting up in the panels.

The third stage is to prevent as much airborne noise as possible from escaping through openings in the compartment and badly fitting hatches and covers. This is easily achieved by the use of a soft rubber strip along all joints between hatch covers. Any other openings can be sealed with the use of expanding spray foam or silicone sealants available from most chandlers. Wiring trunking and control-cable ducting are two areas that will probably require this type of sealing.

A proper sound insulation scheme is a reasonably simple task to undertake, but unfortunately, as we have already seen, the job is complicated by the fact that engines require copious amounts of air for both combustion and cooling purposes and this is where a compromise must be reached with the use of ducted air-intakes so that the engine can breathe but still be restrained vocally.

Obviously some loss of sound-proofing will take place when ducting is introduced into the scheme, but this can be kept within acceptable limits by careful positioning of the inlets and their baffles, which act as sound breaks.

Air inlets and outlets need to be carefully designed and built so that there is no direct route for the sound to travel out: the more tortuous the route the sound must travel, the more it will be absorbed by the sound-proofing on its way out. It is often the case with smaller boats that stainless steel louvre vents are used on the hull sides for engine compartment ventilation with no internal baffles to prevent sound escaping. Not only does this negate the effects of any sound-proofing scheme, it also allows an easy entry for water in rough weather.

To improve both these aspects it is possible to buy or make up simple header boxes to fit inside the vents. From the top of these boxes trunking can be led in a swan-neck down into the engine compartment and covered with sound insulation. The ends should be baffled so that sound cannot enter the trunking directly. It is possible to buy special sound-proofed trunking with the sound-absorbing insulation on the inside. This is specialized material, very expensive and not readily available to the DIY boat owner.

To make up the low-cost sound-proofing mentioned above, each panel must be

battened with 1in x 1in (25mm x 25mm) timber, allowing for the sealing surface where the panel rests on the frame. The corner joints of the battening must be a good fit to maintain the sound-absorption qualities. A heavy coat of bitumastic paint can then be applied to the entire area inside the battens; the heavier it is applied, the more effective it will be in preventing the panels from reverberating.

A 4in (100mm) thick layer of fibre-glass insulation is then cut to fit snugly inside the battens and placed onto the bitumastic layer. A piece of peg-board (or expanded aluminium mesh) is then cut to the outside dimension of the battens to be screwed down all round over

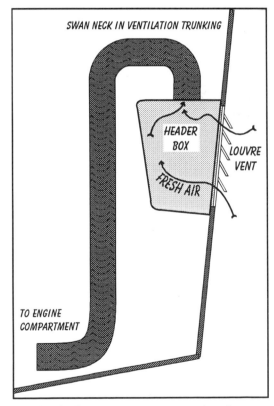

The header box prevents water entering the ventilation trunking while still allowing air to circulate freely.

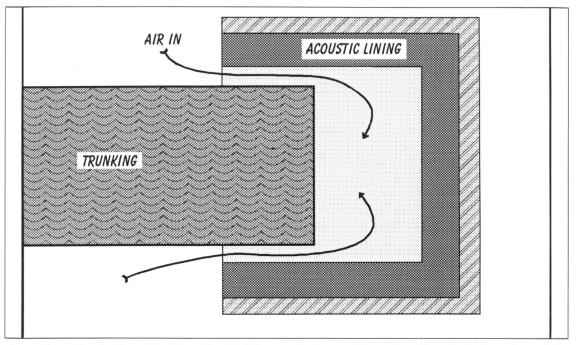

A sound-proofing baffle at the inboard end of the ventilation trunking allows free circulation of air while drastically reducing noise escape because there is no direct line into the trunking.

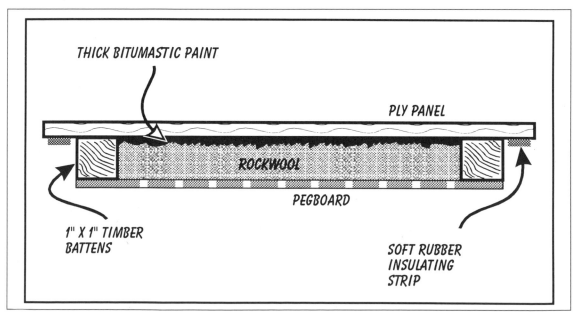

Cross-section of a low-cost sound-proofing panel.

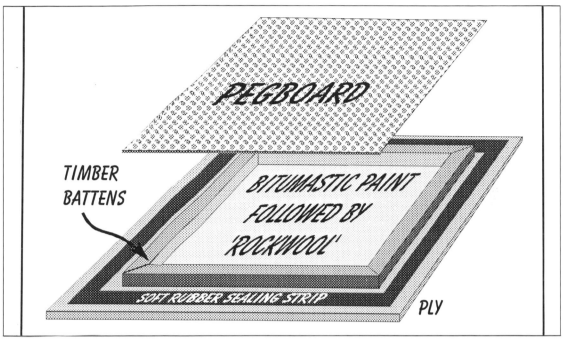

An overview of the same sound-proofing panel.

the insulation. The panel then only needs a strip of soft rubber all round the sealing face before being fitted into place.

Where the sound-proofing is to be fitted to GRP hull sides, the battens can be bonded into position before installing the insulation. To ensure long life, all the bare timber, including both faces of the peg-board, should be sealed before assembly.

When the job is completed, the boat will need to be test run. A vast improvement will immediately be noticed. However, by carefully checking all round the vessel, it may be possible to pinpoint further areas of improvement, perhaps where trunking has inadvertently been left unsealed or where panels are not sitting squarely in place to form a proper seal. As the work becomes more effective it becomes very much easier to find 'sound leaks'. My own criteria for an effective system is when engine noise can be heard emanating from the throttle/gear controls at the helm above the other background engine noises. This noise is transmitted along the control cables, and when this stage is reached I consider the job to have been a success.

PERSHILLA

When building *Pershilla* I installed proprietary brand sound-proofing and sealed each floorboard as it was installed. However, during the repowering project some material had to be removed for running new pipework and wiring, and most of the sound-proofing work was concerned with refitting new sections. I did take the opportunity of replacing all the soft neoprene strips on the sealing faces of the removable floorboards. This material hardens with time and becomes brittle, so losing its effectiveness as a sealing medium.

LAUNCHING, RUNNING AND TESTING

12

PREPARATION

Final preparation for running the engine once the installation work is complete varies depending on the make of engine, but basically it should include a final check of the entire job to ensure that nothing has been forgotten or left disconnected. Items such as the drain plugs in the sump and gearbox should be tested for tightness, while a similar test of all the hose clips on the engine and water system will prevent flooding during start-up. If, like Cummins, the engine manufacturer requires a commissioning trial before validating the warranty the final stage is to book this trial before putting the boat back into commission.

PERSHILLA

Prior to launching, the new four-blade propeller was installed onto the shaft with plenty of waterproof grease. The securing nut was tightened and both shaft and nut were drilled to accept a stainless steel locking split-pin. The last operation in the stern gear area was to change the Ambassador Marine Stripper rope cutter from a three-bladed to a two-bladed version. Having come to rely on this piece of equipment for keeping the propeller unfouled for the last six years I did not intend to forfeit this peace of mind. The reason for changing from three blades to two was to permit the Stripper blades to align with the propeller blades, thus ensuring that the slight water disturbance caused passes harmlessly between the propeller blades without upsetting the smooth flow. In the larger sizes Ambassador supplies four-blade Strippers, but two blades work equally well in the smaller sizes.

Until *Pershilla* was afloat, it was not possible to fill the engine with oil, as the dipstick must be calibrated once the vessel is afloat to allow for the installation angle of the engine. This ensures that the correct amount of oil is added regardless of the installation angle. Once *Pershilla* was afloat, 12 litres of high-quality 15w-40 engine oil was poured through the filler and, after five minutes to allow for draining into the sump, the 'Low' oil level on the dipstick was marked with a DIY engraving tool. Another 2 litres of oil was then added, and after another five minutes the 'High' oil level on the dipstick was marked. Even when installing a used engine it is good practice to follow this procedure to ensure that the correct amount of oil is added.

The Twin Disc gearbox was less fussy and was simply filled with the correct quantity of HD30 engine oil. The cooling system was slowly filled with a 50/50 mixture of ethylene glycol anti-freeze and water to allow air to bleed out of the various parts.

The fuel system was then bled by opening the bleed valve on the fuel filter block and operating the plunger-type manual fuel pump until air-free fuel flowed from the bleed valve. The valve was then closed and the bleed valve on the injection pump opened to allow the same procedure to be followed. The engine was then started for the first time. It was run for about thirty seconds to circulate the engine oil and then stopped and left for a further five minutes to allow the oil to drain back to the sump. This enabled the sump oil level to be topped up to the 'High' mark on the dipstick, ensuring that the system was filled to capacity.

Sea Trials

Cummins' commissioning process is part of the warranty procedure and ensures that the installation complies in every respect with Cummins specifications. Although there are many areas to cover, the installation manual supplied with the engine provided all the information required to complete a successful installation. I was very pleased to use this service, as it would confirm that the installation had indeed been carried out to meet Cummins' specification.

The day of the trial was overcast but calm when the commissioning engineer duly arrived at Gillingham Marina. The first part of the test consisted of a visual inspection of the

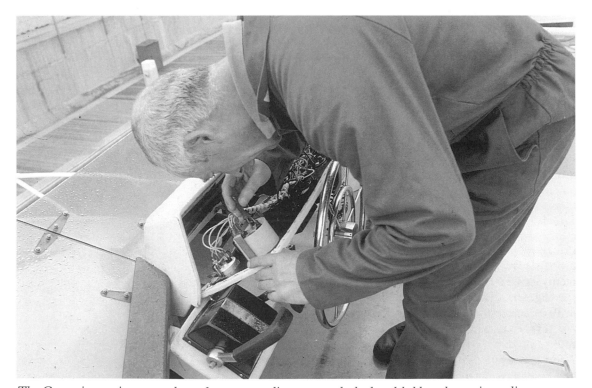

The Cummins engineer sets the tachometer readings to match the hand-held stroboscopic reading.

The test rig being installed on the engine.

installation and a few questions concerning specific areas, while notes for the final written report were taken.

The engine was started to allow a hand-held strobe to be used to read off the true engine revs at mid-throttle. From this reading the alternator-sensed tachometers were set to match in the wheelhouse and on the fly-bridge. The engine was then run up to full throttle in neutral to ensure that it was reaching its proper maximum speed offload.

The next hour was spent by the engineer installing his test rig onto the engine. The main area of concern to me was the engine compartment temperature while running, due to the undersized engine compartment venti-lation inlets. I hoped the three big intake fans fitted to blow cold air into the compartment while the two original extractor fans drew hot air out would be sufficient.

Once the test rig was installed we moved

out of the marina to begin the sea trial. Once past Folly Point the throttle was opened and the first twenty-minute test run was made at 2,200rpm. This was followed by further runs,

The first leg of the test as the engineer makes notes of the various test parameters.

Pershilla running bow high as maximum speed is approached, making it impossible to see over the bow.

The crew retreat to the fly-bridge to see where they are going!

each adding 200rpm to the speed until we had reached maximum revs. Unfortunately we were unable to achieve the full 2,800rpm required by the Cummins specification – the best we could achieve was 2,650rpm; it seemed that the propeller was slightly over-pitched. However, getting to within 150rpm of the predicted shaft speed was pretty good going for a first attempt with a new engine, so I was not unduly disappointed.

The fact that *Pershilla*'s bow was so high in the air that it was impossible to see over the bow from within the wheelhouse was thought to be another contributing factor to the low revs, but it was necessary to retire to the fly-bridge to steer in any case.

Pershilla's top speed was well below the predicted maximum of 12.5 knots, with the best we could achieve being 10.4 knots. However, these were early days and I expected to achieve further improvements with a little more development work. The main task of the day – to commission the engine installation – proved that overall the installation was a complete success, and all that was needed now was a little fine-tuning to enable *Pershilla* to accommodate the ample power now installed.

Fine-Tuning

The next step was to design and fit a pair of fixed trim tabs to get the bow down. The recommended size of tab for the weight and speed of the boat was 48in x 12in (120cm x 30cm). The tabs were fabricated from 4mm mild steel plates with 6mm stiffeners on the top and a 1in (25mm) lip formed into the trailing edge to keep the tabs rigid and give the water a smooth run-off. The tabs were bolted through the hull with 8mm bolts at 9in (230mm) intervals and secured at their initial angle with two, large, galvanized rigging screws. These allowed the angle of the tabs to be adjusted manually once afloat again.

The initial setting for the first test was 5 degrees down on the line of the hull bottom. On a calm day we achieved an across-the-board speed increase of 0.4 knots but no increase in revs. This meant that right through the cruising range at every rev setting the speed was up a little. Although it was less than half a knot it was an increase achieved at no extra fuel cost, so we were already running more efficiently. I then adjusted the tabs down a further 3 degrees,

General view of the steel trim tabs.

The trim tab rigging screws used for making manual adjustments.

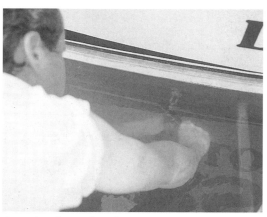

Measuring the length of the rigging screws ensured equal adjustment of each tab.

Screwing down the tabs manually.

Pershilla under way on test. This is what it was all for!

and we tried again. The speed was exactly the same but the revs were slightly down, something I had not expected.

A later test with our rigid inflatable tender removed from the davits produced a further increase in speed up to a best of 11.3 knots. This was quite interesting to note, as I had not really considered the tender's weight as a significant factor. Its position hanging right aft does, however, give the weight some leverage that obviously holds the stern down.

After putting over a hundred running hours on the engine, a further increase in speed has been noticed, together with a matching increase of another 50rpm. This we attribute to the engine freeing up during running-in. Now a maximum speed of 11.3 knots is achieved when fully laden. With the tender removed we have managed an all-time best of 11.7 knots, and during normal running can cruise at a very comfortable 10.5 knots, which is better than we were aiming for.

GLOSSARY

After-cooler Similar in design to a heat exchanger, the after-cooler (or inter-cooler) cools and condenses the compressed intake air from the turbo-charger and further boosts the engine power output.

Cavitation Cavitation is caused by water being displaced from the propeller blades faster than it can be replaced. This forms a vacuum on the surface of the blade that causes in-rushing water molecules to implode against the surface, causing pitting and ultimate failure. It may also be indicated by propeller slip and sudden increased engine revs.

Calorifier A domestic water storage tank with a heating coil within that is fed with hot water from the engine's freshwater cooling system, providing free hot water from the waste heat produced by the engine.

Compression joint A mechanical joint used in pipework to provide a perfect seal that can be opened and resealed many times without losing its effectiveness.

Core plug Also known as expansion plugs, these plugs are fitted into the outer water jacket of the engine block and are designed to push out under the pressure of ice when the engine has frozen due to lack of anti-freeze. This may prevent the block from cracking.

Crimp terminal A cable end fitting that provides the means of making a professional-quality joint. Crimp terminals are available in a variety of sizes and styles to suit different applications. Low-cost kits complete with crimping tool are available from car accessory shops.

Cutless bearing Cutless bearings are water-lubricated rubber bearings designed to minimize shaft wear while offering long life and good abrasion resistance.

Direct cooling Engine cooling where water from the river or sea is pumped directly around the engine block before being expelled; usually via the exhaust.

Direct injection Where the fuel is sprayed directly onto the top of the piston.

Heater plugs A cold start device incorporating a heating coil that screws into every combustion chamber of the engine to warm the air within and assist cold starting. Only used on indirect-injection engines.

Impeller The moving part of a rotary fluid pump. It may be made of metal or a flexible material such as the rubber or nitrile used in raw-water pumps.

Indirect cooling Engine cooling where the water from the river or sea passes through tubes in a heat exchanger that transfers the heat from the fresh water circulating through the block.

Indirect injection Used in engines with pre-combustion chambers.

Injection pump Meters the amount of fuel to be sprayed into the cylinder at any given throttle setting.

Injector Also known as an atomizer, this is a self-sealing valve that atomizes the precise metered amount of fuel and sprays it into the combustion chamber under pressure from the injection pump.

Power-to-weight ratio The output power of an engine compared to its weight. A heavy engine with a low power output has a lower power-to-weight ratio than a lightweight unit with a high power output.

R & D The brand name of R & D Marine, who manufacture a wide range of drive couplings and flexible engine mounting feet. Address can be found in Appendix G.

Raw-water pump Used to draw water from the river or sea for engine cooling; it may be used in both direct and indirect cooled systems.

Sealing ring Also known as an olive. A metal ring, usually made of brass or copper, used to seal a compression pipe joint.

Sump The oil reservoir at the bottom of the engine, usually a pressed steel fabrication.

Thermostart A cold start device mounted in the inlet manifold, utilizing a heating coil that opens a fuel valve to allow fuel onto the coil. The fuel is ignited and the flames are drawn into the cylinders to assist with cold starting. Mainly found in direct injection engines.

Torque In very simply terms, torque is a twisting force, in this case on the gearbox and propeller shaft. The gearbox must be strong enough to withstand the torque produced by the engine and the propeller shaft must be able to withstand the increased torque of a reduction gearbox, designed to slow the revs of the shaft. For a given horsepower and engine speed, high shaft revs equal low torque, low shaft revs equal high torque.

Turbo-charger A turbine-powered air pump driven by exhaust gases that raises the intake pressure to provide greater power output.

Voltage drop The difference between voltage measured at a battery and at the end of a long section of cable.

APPENDIX A

SIZE AND POWER COMPARISON CHARTS

Size/Power/Gearbox Reduction Ratio/Propeller Comparison for Planing and Semi-Displacement Hulls

Water-line length (ft)	Displacement (tons)	Engine power Bhp @ 2,800	Reduction	Prop size (in)	Tip clearance (in)	Speed (knots)
20	3	65	1.5:1	16 x 11	2.4	9.6
20	3	100	1.5:1	15.5 x 15	2.3	16.3
20	3	140	1.5:1	17 x 16	2.5	18.9
20	3	180	1.5:1	17.5 x 18	3.2	21.5
20	3	65	2:1	19 x 16	2.8	10.6
20	3	100	2:1	21 x 18	3.1	16.9
20	3	140	2:1	19 x 20	2.8	18.6
20	3	180	2:1	20 x 24	3.3	22.7
20	3	65	3:1	24 x 22	3.6	11.1
20	3	100	3:1	26 x 27	3.9	18.2
20	3	140	3:1	27 x 32	3.1	21.8
20	3	180	3:1	29 x 37	3.6	24.7
30	5	80	1.5:1	17 x 11	2.5	10.3
30	5	140	1.5:1	18 x 15	2.7	13.5
30	5	80	2	20.5 x 15	3	11.1
30	5	140	2	20 x 20	3	13.9
30	5	200	2	21 x 23	3.1	20.9
30	5	80	3	25.5 x 21	3.8	11.6
30	5	140	3	28 x 29	4.2	19.8
30	5	200	3	30 x 30	4.5	23.1
40	10	80	2	22 x 13	3.3	9.4
40	10	140	2	21.5 x 16	3.2	11.2

40	10	80	2.5	23 x 17	3.4	9.5
40	10	140	2.5	25.7 x 20	3.8	12.1
40	10	200	2.5	24 x 23	3.6	13.4
40	10	250	2.5	24.5 x 27	3.6	15.2
40	10	80	3	26 x 19	3.9	9.7
40	10	140	3	28.5 x 23	4.2	12.3
40	10	200	3	30 x 26	4.5	14.6
40	10	250	3	31 x 31	4.6	16.5
40	12	80	3	26 x 19	3.9	8.9
40	14	80	3	26.5 x 18	3.9	8.4
40	12	140	3	29 x 22	4.3	11.3
40	14	140	3	29.5 x 21	4.4	10.5
40	12	200	3	30 x 25	4.5	13.2
40	14	200	3	31 x 24	4.6	12.2
40	12	250	3	31.5 x 27	4.7	14.8
40	14	250	3	32 x 26	4.8	13.5

Size/Power /Maximum Hull Speed Comparison for Heavy Displacement Hulls

Water-line length (ft)	Displacement (tons)	Engine power Bhp @ 2,800	Speed (knots)
20	3	15	6
25	5	15	6
30	6	23	7
40	14	47	8
40	25	90	8
45	25	120	9
45	30	150	9
50	25	85	9
50	30	105	9

APPENDIX B

CUMMINS ENGINES DUTY RATINGS

Recreation/Light Duty Commercial

(Average Load Factor of 30 per cent or less)

Engines with this rating are intended for powering marine pleasure craft used for personal use only and for powering some marine commercial boats such as gillnetters, bow pickers, skiffs, oil skimmers and small fishing craft. Warranty coverage is different depending upon the actual usage described above.

This power rating is intended for use in variable load applications where full power is limited to one hour out of every eight hours of operation. Also, reduced power operations must be at or below cruise RPM. This rating is an ISO3046 Fuel Stop Power Rating and is for applications that operate less than 750 hours per year.

Medium Continuous Rating

(Average Load Factor of 30–70 per cent)

Engines with this rating are intended for powering commercial boats such as lobster boats, crew boats, party fishing boats, charter fishing boats, long range cruisers, harbour and coastal patrol boats, search and rescue boats, fire boats, bay shrimpers, clam boats, crab boats and seine skiffs.

This power rating is intended for continuous use in variable load applications where full power is limited to six hours out of every twelve hours of operation. Also, reduced power operations must be at or below cruise RPM. This rating is an ISO3046 Fuel Stop Power Rating and is for applications that operate less than 3,000 hours per year.

Continuous Rating

(Average Load Factor greater than 70 per cent)

Engines with this rating are intended for powering commercial boats such as buoy tenders, research vessels, offshore supply boats, fishing trawlers, purse seiners, tugs, tow boats and car passenger ferries.

This power rating is intended for continuous use in applications requiring uninterrupted service at full power. This rating is an

ISO3046 Standard Power Rating and the SAE J1228 Continuous Crankshaft Power Rating.

Note: The above ratings refer to the American market and therefore describe American boats. However, it is fairly easy to deduce the UK equivalent, while Cummins UK will recommended the type of engine and duty rating for any type of vessel.

APPENDIX C

CUMMINS RECOMMENDED ENGINE COMPARTMENT VENTILATION CROSS-SECTIONAL AREA FOR GIVEN HORSE-POWER.

Engine BHP	Minimum recommended ventilation area (sq in)
64	35
76	38
80	41
130	59
150	73
180	122
210	135
250	140
300	170
400	214

The above figures vary slightly depending on the cubic capacity of the engine and its maximum operating revs.

Note: On *Pershilla* the eight 3in engine compartment vents totalled a maximum area of 56.5 sq in, a shortfall of 113 sq in on the 170 sq in required from the above table. The use of forced air ventilation using intake fans overcame this problem without the need for drastic rebuilding of the ventilation ducting.

*A*PPENDIX *D*

WET EXHAUST DIAMETER FOR GIVEN HORSE-POWER.

Engine BHP	Wet Exhaust Diameter (in)
80	3
150	3.5
180	4
250	5
300	6
400	8

Note: The above sizes may need to be increased where a long exhaust run is required or when a lift silencer is installed. For dry exhausts the size may often be reduced.

*A*PPENDIX *E*

MINIMUM RAW WATER PIPING AND FILTER SIZES FOR GIVEN HORSE-POWER.

Engine BHP	Raw water piping size (in)
210	1.25
250	1.5
400	2.0

Note: The pipe-work should correspond to the size of the raw water pump inlet and outlet sizes. The water strainer, sea cocks and valves should also match this size.

APPENDIX F

BATTERY CAPACITY FOR GIVEN HORSE-POWER IN CCA. (COLD CRANKING AMPS)

Engine BHP	Battery Capacity 12 volt	Battery Capacity 24 volt
150	800 CCA	400 CCA
250	950 CCA	475 CCA
300	1100 CCA	475 CCA
400	1800 CCA	900 CCA

Note: As engine size increases so does the requirement for starting battery capacity. It is easy to see why large engines are equipped with 24 volt starting due to the enormous CCA rating required on a 12 volt system.

APPENDIX G

USEFUL ADDRESSES

Adverc BM (alternator regulators, all on-board battery charging equipment)
245 Trysull Road
Merry Hill
Wolverhampton WV3 7LG
Tel: 01902 380494

CJR Propulsion (propellers/shafts)
72 Quayside Road
Bitterne Manor
Southampton SO18 1AD
Tel: 01703 222032

Countrose Engineering (water-lubricated rubber bearings)
Unit 26
Derby Trading Estate
Stores Road
Derby DE21 4BE
Tel: 01332 340471

Cummins Diesel
Rutherford Drive
Park Farm South
Wellingborough
Northamptonshire NN8 6AN
Tel: 01933 672200

D. W. Davies (stainless steel fabrications)
Unit 7
Charfleets House
Charfleets Industrial Estate
Canvey Island
Essex SS8 4PW
Tel: 01268 684473

Gillingham Marina
173 Pier Road
Gillingham
Kent ME7 1UB
Tel: 01634 280022

Halyard Marine (exhaust systems, shaft couplings, shaft seals)
Whaddon Business Park
Southampton Road
Whaddon
Wiltshire SP5 3HF
Tel: 01722 710922

Marine and Industrial Transmissions Ltd
(Twin Disc gearboxes)
Queenborough Shipyard
South Street
Queenborough
Kent ME11 5AL
Tel: 01795 580808

R and D Marine Couplings
Clothall Road
Baldock
Hertfordshire SG7 6PG
Tel: 01462 892391

INDEX